FANTASTIC
JESUS

FANTASTIC JESUS

LAW EMEKA MODEME

Printed in the United States of America

First printing, 2020

ISBN 13: 9781999884734

Ameze Resources Limited

18 Torcross Road
Manchester

M9 0GP

England, United Kingdom

www.amezeresources.com

Email: Law@amezeresources.co

Lawmodeme@yahoo.co.uk

DEDICATION

To all seekers of knowledge, enlightenment and truth

TABLE OF CONTENTS

PREFACE

This book is one volume of the result of a scrupulous research that lasted many years on the religious doctrine of human salvation – the *raison d'etre* of the Abrahamic faiths. Because I was born into a strong Christian home, and grew up as a Christian, I fully believed in the Bible and in Jesus, as the Son of God and Saviour of humanity. I had no doubt that the gospels were true, and that Jesus Christ was the only way to salvation, God and heaven. I believed like other Christians that non-Christians, unless they repented and accepted Jesus as their Lord and Saviour, would be condemned to everlasting suffering in Hell Fire. I was not merely a churchgoer – I preached the gospel whenever I had the opportunity to do so with a view to 'winning Souls' for Christ.

However, I had misgivings about many of the doctrines of Christianity, and these grew stronger as I became older, wiser, and more exposed to other peoples and religions of the world. Of particular concern to me was the doctrine of salvation, which I could not reconcile with my belief in the universality of God and the oneness of humanity. I could not understand why only Christians would go to heaven when most of the people in the world are not Christians. I also found it difficult to understand the Christian position that only the Bible could be the Word of God when other religions have their own Holy Scriptures that adherents sincerely believe came from God. I could not come to terms with the notion that otherwise good people would be condemned to eternity of suffering in Hell Fire because they did not accept Christ, while notoriously bad people could receive salvation because they accepted Jesus as Lord and Saviour, even if this was at the point of death.

To me, the idea of salvation through Christ alone seemed unjust and unfair to people who were born into non-Christian homes, because I could easily have been a Muslim, Hindu, Sikh, or Jew, or an adherent of any other religion. I could also have been an atheist, a 'pagan' or an agnostic if I had been born into a different family, part of the world or set of circumstances. This is particularly poignant in my country Nigeria were roughly half of the population are Muslims, most of whom fervently believe in the message of Allah as transmitted by Mohammed His prophet. The religious divisions in the country have often manifested in bloody persecutions, conflicts and acts of terrorism.

It also troubled me that my ancestors were neither Christians nor Muslims but had different perceptions of spirituality and God. Were these people lost? Did they not know God? If the Christian God and His salvation was the only way, why did He not manifest to my ancestors for the thousands of years they lived before the arrival of Christianity? Conversely, if Islam is the way, why did Allah not bring His massage to my ancestors or to those living presently in the part of the country where I was born? I also wondered why Jews, from whose midst Jesus Christ arose, were largely not Christians.

Despite my misgivings, however, I believed that at the core, there was substance and truth in the gospels. Even if many have twisted and manipulated them for selfish and evil ends, the problem, I believed, could not be with Jesus but with those purporting to be his followers. I believed that in the life and ministry of Jesus would be the essential ingredients for universal love, unity and peace. I was determined to bring these out by a scrupulous study of the Bible and the research of sundry Christian and religious authorities. The effort has been greatly rewarding and revealing, even if very challenging.

This volume, which deals with the life, times, ministry, death, resurrection and ascension of Jesus Christ, contain information and materials hidden, albeit in plain sight, from the masses for over two thousand years. The purpose of the book is to enlighten and educate. I have endeavoured to present the information in a manner accessible to the ordinary reader while maintaining the highest standards of scholarship. It should therefore appeal to everyone who seeks information, knowledge and truth on the subject.

INTRODUCTION

For unto us a child is born, unto us a son is given, and the government will be upon His shoulders. And He will be called Wonderful Counsellor, Mighty God, Everlasting Father, Prince of Peace. - Isaiah 9: 6-7

With about two billion adherents and numerous denominations, Christianity is statistically the largest religion in the world. In modern times, it has arguably wielded the greatest influence in people's lives, and in global politics. Although the number of believers is falling drastically in its homeland of Europe, Christianity continues to rise in some other parts of the world, especially Africa, the USA and South America. At present, Africa - of all continents - has the largest number of Christians, and it is projected to consolidate this position in the coming decades. The rise of Christianity in Africa coincides with the emergence of so-called Pentecostal denominations that have pulled many members from the Roman Catholic Church, the Anglican Church, and other traditional denominations.

Whatever the denomination, Christians put their faith and hope for salvation on Jesus Christ. Most see Jesus as God incarnate—the second member of the Divine Trinity—and the co-creator of the universe. They believe that he miraculously came down from heaven to sacrifice himself for the salvation of humanity that had severed itself from divine grace because of the sin of the first humans. Jesus' mission was to reconcile humans with God. Christianity fundamentally teaches that belief in, and acceptance of, Jesus as Lord and Saviour would lead to salvation and eternal life in heaven; while unbelief or rejection would condemn the stubborn soul to everlasting suffering in Hell Fire.

The only source of significant information about the life, times and ministry of Jesus Christ is the Bible's New Testament, which testimonies Christians regard as incontrovertible. They believe that Jesus came in fulfilment of prophesies contained in the Bible's Old Testament. They believe that he preached a message of salvation and performed numerous extraordinary miracles in the course of a ministry that lasted about three years. They also believe that Jesus rose from the dead and ascended to heaven after Roman government authorities, at the instigation of Jewish leaders, had crucified him. From heaven, they insist that Jesus would return to earth to take with him those who believe in his name and accept him as Lord and Saviour.

However, are these claims about Jesus Christ true? Are they factual and historically correct? This book takes a close, objective, critical and analytical look at the story of Jesus Christ as told in the Bible and elaborated in Christian literature, doctrines and practices. With solid biblical, secular and scholarly authority, it answers the most critical questions about Jesus Christ and compares his story with those of the protagonists of other religions, both ancient and modern. The result is astonishing.

The reader is invited to proceed with an open mind, and discover whether the story of Jesus Christ rests on facts and history, or whether it is rooted in religious mythology. In other words, is Jesus Christ fantastic in the sense of being the wonderful Counsellor, Mighty God and Prince of Peace? Or is he fantastic in the sense of being fanciful or unreal?

CHAPTER 1

WAS JESUS CONCEIVED BY THE HOLY SPIRIT AND BORN BY A VIRGIN?

Therefore, the Lord himself will give you a sign: The virgin will conceive and give birth to a son, and will call him Immanuel. – Isaiah 7:14

At the core of Christianity is the belief that its supposed founder and hero, Jesus Christ,[1] was God who incarnated as a human being via a supernatural conception in order to accomplish the salvation of humanity. After upsetting Jewish authorities with his teaching and doing many wondrous things, he was murdered in a conspiracy involving Jewish leaders and the Roman government. It is believed, however, that Jesus defeated death and ascended to heaven from where he had come. These events, Christianity claims, elevate Jesus above the founders of other religions who were mere human beings, and who - when they died - stayed dead like all mortals. Are these claims about Jesus true? The conception and birth of Jesus Christ constitute the foundation on which rests the

---

[1] The Bible's New Testament uses the title 'Christ' as part of the personal name of Jesus, said to be of Nazareth. So, throughout the book, 'Jesus' is used interchangeably with 'Jesus Christ' or 'Christ'.

other claims about his life, ministry, death, resurrection and ascension, as well as the claim that he is the Saviour of the world. Is this foundation solid enough to carry the super-structure?

The Gospel Story

The story of the conception of Jesus Christ appears only in the gospels of Matthew and Luke. According to Luke's gospel, God sent Angel Gabriel to Mary, the betrothed of Joseph. The angel told her that she was highly favoured and would conceive a son whom she should call Jesus. Mary questioned the angel on how this could be, given that she was still a virgin. The angel explained that the Holy Spirit and the power of God would overshadow her so that the child she would conceive would be the Son of God. Mary accepted this explanation and prophecy with praise worship to God.[2]

After Jesus' birth in Bethlehem, (Joseph and Jesus' mother had moved to the town shortly before the birth), Luke reports that an angel of God appeared on a certain night to some shepherds who were watching over their flock nearby. The angels assured the shepherds that they had brought good news of the birth of a Saviour, whom they would find lying in a manger wrapped in clothes. Suddenly, a great company of 'the heavenly host' appeared and together with the angels, sang praises to God. When the angels (and the heavenly host) had gone back into heaven, the shepherds hurried off and presently found Mary and the child Jesus lying in a manger, as they had been told. Rejoicing

---

[2] Luke 1: 26 - 56.

and praising God, the shepherds spread the news of these glorious events to all and sundry.[3]

On its part, Matthew's gospel narrates that Mary, the betrothed of Joseph, became pregnant 'through the Holy Spirit' before she could consummate her relationship with her husband. However, Joseph - not wishing to expose Mary to public ridicule - decided to divorce her quietly. Then an angel of God appeared to him in a dream and encouraged him to keep Mary as his wife because her pregnancy was the result of the work of the Holy Spirit. Joseph accepted Mary and the pregnancy, avoided any sexual contact with her until she delivered, and then named the child 'Jesus', as the angel had instructed.[4] Matthew goes on to claim[5] that the above events took place in fulfilment of the prophecy in Isaiah 7:14 that, 'the virgin will conceive and give birth to a son, and they will call him "Immanuel" (which means "God with us").'

Matthew's gospel[6] further claims that Jesus was born in a house in the town of Bethlehem in Judea, in fulfilment of the prophecy in Micah 5:2; that, although Bethlehem was a small tribe in Judah, out of it 'will come for me one who will be ruler over Israel, whose origins are from of old, from ancient times'. After Jesus' birth, a star signalled the time and location to some Magi 'from the east'[7] who followed it to

---

[3] See Luke 2:1-27.
[4] See Matthew 1: 18 - 25.
[5] Matthew 1:23
[6] See Matthew 2.
[7] Magi are 'wise men' or astrologers; the East here probably signifies Persia.

Jerusalem and enquired where the 'future king' was born. When the news of this enquiry reached King Herod, he and all his subjects were disturbed. Upon enquiry as to where 'the Christ' would be born, Herod summoned the Magi and sent them to Bethlehem with instructions to find the child and report to him, so that he might go and worship too. The Magi then left Herod and, guided by the same star that had led them to Jerusalem, traced the child Jesus to Bethlehem, and the exact house where he was born. On seeing the child, they worshipped and presented him with the gifts of gold, frankincense and myrrh. However, following a warning in a dream, the Magi departed without reporting to Herod.

When Herod realised that he had been outwitted, he ordered the slaughter of every boy who was two years old or below in Bethlehem and its vicinity, apparently in fulfilment of the prophecy in Jeremiah 31:15.[8] By this time, however, following an angelic warning, Joseph had fled to Egypt with Mary and the infant Jesus. The family stayed in Egypt until the death of Herod and an instruction by an angel to return to Israel. This was also apparently in fulfilment of a prophecy in Hosea 11:1 that, 'out of Egypt I have called my son'. However, because Archelaus, Herod's son had succeeded him to the throne, Joseph decided to move his family to the city of Nazareth and settle there in order to avoid the possibility of a repeat of Herod's action.[9]

---

[8] 'A voice was heard in Ramah; wailing and loud lamentation, Rachel weeping for her children; she refuses to be consoled, because they are no more'.
[9] See Matthew 2.

The settlement of the family of Jesus in Nazareth was said to be in fulfilment of the prophecy that, 'He will be called a Nazarene.'[10]

Problems with the Story

The accounts of the conception and birth of Jesus in the gospels of Matthew and Luke contain many inconsistencies, differences, and contradictions that seriously negate their veracity. Some of these are discussed below.

The Angelic Visitation and Joseph

The gospels contradict each other as to whom Angel Gabriel appeared to and when. Whereas, in Luke the angel appears to *Mary before the conception*, but did not appear to Joseph, in Matthew, he appeared to *Joseph after the conception*, but did not appear to Mary. Then, the reaction of Joseph in Matthew is curious when one considers the Jewish law, which he was bound to obey, not only for his own sake, but also for the sake of the whole nation of Israel. Under this law, if a betrothed woman has sexual relationship with a man other than with her husband, the husband is required to send her back to her family where she would be stoned to death, unless her parents could provide to the elders proof of her virginity. This is because the people must 'purge such evil' from amongst them.[11] Although, by Matthew's account, Mary did not have any sexual relations with another man, Joseph did not know that. He believed that Mary had betrayed him, but he did not want to disgrace her publicly. Joseph's failure to obey

---

[10] Matthew 2:23.
[11] Deuteronomy 22: 13-21.

the law as stated above would have been a flagrant violation of the law of God, as he believed it, especially giving the incredulity of the 'Holy Spirit' conception.

However, contrary to Matthew's story, in Luke, there was no mention of Joseph's reaction to the pregnancy; and Mary was not concerned about how he might react. Curiously, though, Mary questioned the possibility of her becoming pregnant even though she already had a husband. If the account of Luke were to be accepted, one would have to wonder what the reaction of Joseph and his people might have been. Would Joseph not have felt obliged to send Mary back to her parents for stoning as the Bible commands, especially as he received no explanation for the strange pregnancy? Would the elders not have been equally obliged in the circumstances to execute the punishment in order to 'purge' the evil from their land?

False Reliance on Virgin Prophecy

The claim that Jesus' birth was in fulfilment of the prophecy in Isaiah about virgin birth is false, even though it contributed to the Catholic dogma of Perpetual Virginity of Mary.[12] The reference to 'virgin' in Isaiah 7:14 was an apparent mistranslation of the word *almah*, which simply means 'young woman' in the Hebrew Bible, to *Parthenos,* which means 'virgin' in its Greek version.[13] However, even if *almah*

---

[12] The dogma teaches that Mary was a virgin before, during, and after the conception and birth Jesus. See *The Catholic Encyclopaedia*, http://www.newadvent.org/cathen/15448a.htm.

[13] See *The New Oxford Annotated Bible, NRSV with the Apocrypha* (4thed) (Oxford University Press 2010) 978 (italics in original). See also, *The Jewish Encyclopaedia,*

means the same thing as 'virgin', this would not suggest a virgin conception or birth. Although under the Law of Moses, all young Jewish women are required - at the pain of death by stoning - to be virgins at the time of their marriage,[14] they still got pregnant through natural sexual intercourse with their spouses.

In any case, the passage did not concern the conception of Jesus at all. The events referred to in the 'prophecy' apparently took place around 734 BC, many centuries before the birth of Jesus. The combined military forces of the kings of Israel and Syria (Aram) had converged against Judah and its young king, Ahaz, such that 'the hearts of Ahaz and his people were shaken, as the trees of the forest are shaken by the wind.'[15] In the light of this development, Prophet Isaiah went to give assurances to king Ahaz that Yahweh would protect him and his kingdom from the forces that had assembled against them. As a sign of this, the prophet informed the king that, the 'young woman' would bear a son whom she would call Immanuel. The prophet went on to say that before the child would be old enough to eat curd and honey and before he could differentiate right from wrong, Israel and Syria would have suffered destruction and desertion.[16] The 'sign' therefore referred to an imminent physical delivery from military forces; the woman that would have the child was either the wife of King Ahaz or

---

http://www.jewishencyclopedia.com/articles/10729-messiah.
[14] See Deuteronomy 22:13-21.
[15] Isaiah 7:2.
[16] See Isaiah 7:14-17; WRF Browning (ed.) *Oxford Dictionary of the Bible* (Oxford University Press 2009) 99.

Isaiah; and the child to be born belonged to one of them.[17] Whatever the case might be, the child in question was to be born soon after the prophecy – certainly during the lifetime of King Ahaz and Isaiah. The child could not have been Jesus, whose birth came over seven hundred years later, and the 'virgin' could not have been his mother.

Moreover, although the prophecy clearly stated that the name of the child in question would be 'Immanuel', nobody in the Bible ever called Jesus by that name. In fact, the Isaiah prophecy appears to contradict the message of Angel Gabriel during his visitation to Mary (or Joseph) that the child's name would be 'Jesus'. Furthermore, the related prophecy in Isaiah 9:6-7 that, the child born would be called *wonderful counsellor, mighty God, everlasting father*, and *prince of peace* that would reign forever, was a prophetic expression of the hope of Israelites for the emergence of an anointed mundane king who would deliver them from oppression and restore peace, justice and righteousness. It was not a reference to Jesus, whose expected kingship was heavenly and spiritual.[18]

False Reliance on other Prophecies

The other claims by Matthew that Jesus' conception and birth fulfilled Old Testament prophecies are also completely unfounded. The passage in Micah 5:2 was about the restoration of Israel through the dominion of the House of David. Jesus though was never a king of

---

[17] See WRF Browning (ed.) supra n 16, 157.
[18] See J Barton and J Muddiman (eds.) *The Oxford Bible Commentary* (Oxford University Press 2007) 447 and Chapter 13.

Israel or Judah, and was not of the House of David. The statement in Hosea 11:1 that, 'out of Egypt I called my son' refers to the people of Israel as a whole in relation to their delivery from Egypt, and not to Jesus.[19] Similarly, the prophecy in Jeremiah 31:15 about mourning and weeping in Ramah by Rachel has nothing to do with Jesus. That passage relates to Rachel, the wife of Jacob, whose twelve sons supposedly make up the tribes of Israel. The weeping was apparently due to the taking of the tribes of Israel into exile by the Assyrians in 722 BCE.[20] It is not a reference at all to any weeping due to any massacre by Herod of infant children in the blind pursuit of baby Jesus several hundred years later.

Finally, the 'Nazarene prophecy' cited by Matthew, as being fulfilled by Jesus does not exist in the Old Testament. Besides, the term 'Nazarene' does not refer to a town or city, and certainly not to Nazareth.[21] Rather, it refers to a sect of early Christians, notably in Syria.[22] In fact, an angel reportedly referred to Jesus as a Nazarene after his resurrection,[23] while Apostle Paul faced an accusation of being a ringleader of the Nazarene sect.[24] It would seem that the gospel writers had conflated Nazareth with Nazarene. There was no mention of Nazareth in the Old Testament by ancient Jewish

---

[19] See *The New Oxford Annotated Bible, NRSV with the Apocrypha* (4[th]ed) supra n 13, 1271.

[20] Ibid, 1109-10.

[21] Ibid, 1750. See also J Barton and J Muddiman (eds.), supra n 18, 850; *Catholic Encyclopaedia,* http://www.newadvent.org.

[22] See *the* WRF Browning (ed.) supra n 16, 265.

[23] Mark 16:6.

[24] See Acts 24:5

historians – or in Jewish writings – as a city, town or village in Galilee. In fact, the first references to that 'city' in the Bible were in connection with Jesus.[25]

However, even if there were a place called Nazareth at the time of Jesus, it would be more a hamlet of between 300 and 500 people than a town or city.[26] Such a hamlet could not have boasted a temple (where the infant Jesus was presented),[27] a synagogue (where Jesus preached),[28] and a crowd of people[29] as alluded in the gospels. Moreover, everybody in the hamlet would have known Jesus. Accordingly, the story of Jesus' miraculous conception, the Magi (or shepherds, according to Luke) visitation, the miraculous escape from Herod's assassination attempt, the flight to and from Egypt, his presentation at the temple accompanied by the song of Simeon the priest (the *Nunc Dimittis*)[30] and Jesus' scriptural precocity at age twelve[31] would have been common knowledge. If these were the case, and given that Jesus would have grown up and lived all his life in the locality, is it not incredible that the people of Nazareth would not only

---

[25] See Luke 2:39; 4:16-30. See also *The Catholic Encyclopaedia*, http://www.newadvent.org/cathen/10725a.htm.

[26] For more on this, see WRF Browning (ed.) supra n 16; *The Catholic Encyclopaedia*, http://www.newadvent.org/cathen/10725a.htm. See also K Humphreys, *Jesus Never Existed: The Tragic Fabrication of a Saviour of the World* (NineBanded Books.com; Jesusneverexisted.com); *The Jewish Encyclopaedia*, http://www.jewishencyclopedia.com/articles/11394-nazareth, *The Encyclopaedia Britannica*, http://www.britannica.com/place/Nazareth-Israel.

[27] Luke 2:22-39.

[28] Luke 4:16, 28.

[29] See Luke 4:30.

[30] See Luke 2:22-24.

[31] See Luke 2:46-47.

reject Jesus but would also try to throw him down to his death from a cliff, as the Bible indicates?[32]

Visit of the Magi

The alleged visitation of the Magi - who were Zoroastrian priests, astrologers or magicians from the Kingdom of Persia (present day Iran)[33] - seems dubious. Why would these people trek 1700 miles from their country over several months[34] in order to worship a future king of the Jews to whom they would owe no allegiance, especially given the fact that Israel was a minor nation relative to Persia? Why would they be overjoyed at the birth of a future king of the Jews and present him with precious gifts? Why would the Magi ask for human direction to the location of the infant Jesus when a star had led them all the way from their own country to Jerusalem and subsequently to the child? Moreover, given that it would have taken them several months to get to Bethlehem from their homeland,[35] they could not have met an infant Jesus.

Luke's gospel confirms the above doubts. Contrary to the account in Matthew about the Magi visitation, Luke claims that local shepherds had visited the infant Jesus, following divine information. These shepherds received no guidance from any star and did not present any gifts to the child Jesus. The story of the Magi homage appears

---

[32] See Luke 4:24-30. See also, K Humphries, *Nazareth: the Town that Theology Built*, http://www.jesusneverexisted.com/nazareth.html.
[33] See *The Catholic Encyclopaedia*,
http://www.newadvent.org/cathen/09527a.htm.
[34] See http://distanceroad.com/bethlehem-to-persia-distance-by-road.
[35] Ibid.

reminiscent of the Old Testament fable of Balaam – a magus from the east – who prophesied blessings and greatness for Israel rather than the curses King Balak of Moab sent him to pronounce.[36] Thus, apart from this incident, there is no indication that these or any other Magi, or people from the east, paid any attention to Jesus throughout his life.

Herod's Slaughter of Infants

It is highly unlikely that King Herod slaughtered all male children from two years down in an attempt to eliminate the infant Jesus. In the first place, Herod was not the king of Judea at the relevant time, so he could not have done the act. He was born in 73 BC and reigned from 37 BC to 4 BC when he died – before the supposed birth of Jesus.[37] Secondly, it is not logical for Herod to embark on the infanticide when he could easily have traced, isolated and killed Jesus any time. Why was he in a hurry to slaughter all male infants based on the words of strangers when he had plenty of time to investigate and deal with the matter? Why would he trust and wait on the visiting Magi to discover the child and report to him if he was so intent on destroying him?

If Herod did indeed commit the infanticide, why did other gospel writers not say a word about it? Would such a horrendous crime not be firmly entrenched in the minds of the people, especially those who were to become Christians, as an indelible reminder of the birth of Jesus? Besides, if such a massacre did take place, would Jewish and

---

[36] See Numbers 23: 1-12; J Barton and J Muddiman (eds.) supra n 18, 849.

[37] See https://www.britannica.com/biography/Herod-king-of-Judaea.

Roman historians not record it?[38] Yet, there is no mention of such an occurrence in any Jewish or Roman historical records, even though there were records of lesser atrocities committed by Herod.[39] Although Herod was notorious for killing many people, including his rivals and family members, the mass murder of babies is not something history would gloss over as the Catholic Encyclopaedia suggests.[40] Confirming the implausibility of the story is the fact that Herod's executioners did not kill John the Baptist even though he was about six months old at the time of Jesus' birth. Instead, Antipater, the son and one the successors of Herod at the request of his wife, killed an adult John.[41] Moreover, Herod took no further steps to kill Jesus, even though he must have realised that the child survived his earlier attempt. This purported plot by Herod to eliminate Jesus is similar to hero stories in the mythology of some even more ancient religions.[42]

Finally, it is doubtful that the birth of a future king would unduly trouble Herod and his subjects. For the Jews who had been expecting a king and deliverer from the house of David, the news of the birth of the future king in the town of David heralded by a star and the reverence of foreign wise men would have been a matter of excitement

---

[38] See Chapter 12.
[39] See WRF Browning, supra n 16, 146-147, 160; *The Catholic Encyclopaedia*, http://www.newadvent.org/cathen/07289c.htm.
[40] See e.g., *The Catholic Encyclopaedia*, http://www.newadvent.org/cathen/07289c.htm, where it is claimed that, 'cruel as the slaughter may appear to us, it disappears among the cruelties of Herod. It cannot, then, surprise us that history does not speak of it'.
[41] See Matthew 14:1-13.
[42] See Chapter 3.

and joy. For Herod, although he was reputed to be a wicked ruler who eliminated his opponents, the birth of a child who might be king many decades in the future should not be a matter of worry or immediate concern, when he would most probably not be alive by that time. Even if he were to be concerned about the retention of the kingship in his family, he would have had plenty of time to deal with the situation. However, given that Israel and Judea were under the dominion of the Roman emperor who determined the political authority of the area, it is unlikely that a supposed future Jewish king unrecognised by the emperor would perturb Herod. In any case, upon the death of Herod, his three sons – Archelaus, Antipas and Phillip – shared the governorship of his domain.

One Event, Different Stories

Apart from the differences already noted between the narratives in the two gospels, Luke also differs from Matthew on other important details. There was no indication in Luke that the baby Jesus was in any danger; neither was there any massacre of innocent baby boys by a jealous King Herod. There was no escape of Jesus and his family to Egypt as claimed by Matthew. Instead, the parents of Jesus lived in the city of Nazareth prior to his birth but had to travel to Bethlehem for a mandatory census that took place in the whole world during the reign of Emperor Caesar Augustus, when Quirinius (Cyrenius) was the governor of Syria. This census apparently required people to travel to their ancestral homes for the counting.[43] It was while they were in

---

[43] Luke 2:1-6.

Bethlehem that Mary gave birth to Jesus. In addition, unlike Matthew who says that Jesus was born in a house, Luke says that he was born in a manger because there was no room in any of the inns in the town.[44]

It is unlikely though, that this worldwide census did in fact take place, as no account exists of it in Roman historical records. Even if a census did take place throughout the Roman Empire, it would not have included Galilee, which was not a Roman province at that time. Furthermore, although Luke claims that the census took place at a time when Quirinius was the governor of the province of Syria, this appears inaccurate since – according to Matthew – Herod was the king of Judea at that time. However, Herod was not the king during the reign of Quirinius. The Jewish historian Josephus in fact records that the census took place during the reign of Archelaus, Herod's son. This census, which did not correspond with the birth of Jesus, was for tax purposes, and did not require people to return to their ancestral homes, and sparked a Jewish uprising.[45] In any case, it is implausible that Joseph would travel about 160 kilometres on foot or donkey to Bethlehem,[46] not because it was his town, but because it was, 'the town of David' and 'he belonged to the house and line of David'.[47]

---

[44] Luke 2: 7.

[45] See, F Josephus, *Antiquities of the Jews* (Acheron Press 2012) Book 18, Chapter 1:1; Acts 5:37; J Barton and J Muddiman (eds.) supra n 18, 928-929; IM Zeitlin. supra n 51, ch. 1, 126. *The Jewish Encyclopaedia*, http://www.jewishencyclopedia.com/articles/4171-census.

[46] The distance between Nazareth and Bethlehem is about 160 KM and would have taken between 8 and 10 days to trek. See http://jesustrail.com/blog/hiking-the-nativity-trail-from-nazareth-to-bethlehem.

[47] See Luke 2:4.

Yet, Luke 2:3 reports that for the census, 'everyone went to their *own town* to register'.[48] Why would Joseph go back twenty-eight generations to the home of David, in order to register?[49] Why did he not go to his own town or the town of his father, grandfather or even great-grand father? Why would he take a heavily pregnant woman on a long foot or donkey journey all that distance? This story appears to be a desperate attempt, somehow, to link Jesus to King David.[50]

No Conception or Birth in the Gospels of Mark and John

Mark, the earliest gospel[51] and which probably provided most of the information used by the other synoptic gospels, begins with the ministry of John the Baptist and the adult baptism of Jesus. Similarly, even though it was written much later than Matthew and Luke, the gospel of John does not say anything on the conception either. Given that John is the gospel most interested in promoting the divinity of Jesus, it is curious that the writer would leave out such an apparently divine and unprecedented occurrence if it did happen. Since Mark and John would not deliberately leave out the story, a logical inference would be that the writers of both gospels were unaware of it. In fact, the picture painted by John concerning the origins of Jesus is very different from that given by Matthew and Luke. Claiming that Jesus

---

[48] Emphasis added.
[49]See Mathew 1; and Luke 3: 23 – 37.
[50] See Chapter 2 for a more detailed discussion of this point.
[51] See the commentary on Mark's gospel in AS Peake, *et al,* (eds.) *A Commentary on the Bible* (Nelson and Sons Ltd Edinburgh 1937). See also, J Barton and J Muddiman (eds.) supra n 18, 928-929; WRF Browning (ed.) supra n 16, 213.

was essentially God, with neither conception nor birth, the gospel declares:

> *In the beginning was the Word, and the Word was with God, and the Word was God. He was with God in the beginning. Through him all things were made; without him nothing was made that has been made. In Him was life, and that life was the light of all mankind. The light shines on in the darkness, and the darkness has not overcome it [...].14 The Word became flesh and made his dwelling among us. We have seen his glory, the glory of the one and only Son, who came from the Father, full of grace and truth.*[52]

Although in other places, John appears to suggest that Jesus was the son of Joseph through Mary, it gives no indication that there was anything extraordinary or unnatural about it.[53]

No Conception or Birth in Paul's Epistles

Apostle Paul, whose epistles pre-date all the canonical gospels and were the first to document and propagate Christian doctrines, did not also narrate the supernatural birth of Jesus.[54] A contemporary of Jesus – having, according to the Bible, been at the forefront of the persecution of the earliest followers of Christ[55] – Paul would have been uniquely placed to have a good knowledge of the conception, birth and infancy story of Jesus. Paul was also one of the foremost missionaries of the early church, and supposedly dealt with the foremost disciples of Jesus. If this story is well-founded or known,

---

[52] See John 1:1-5, 14.
[53] See John 1:45; 6:42; 19:25.

[54] See J Barton and J Muddiman (eds) supra n 18, 1062.
[55] See Acts 7:57; 8:1-3; 1 Corinthians 15:9.

few writers apart from Paul would have been better placed, and would have had a greater need, to narrate it. As the New Testament of the Bible did not yet exist, and there were no other Christian scriptures for the instruction and indoctrination of Gentiles, Paul would have had every reason to detail the supernatural circumstances surrounding the conception and birth of Jesus in his earliest epistles. Yet, he did not do so.

On the contrary, in the few instances where he made passing references to the birth of Jesus, Paul suggested a regular conception and birth rather than a supernatural and mysterious one. For example, in Galatians 4:4, he stated that, 'when the time had fully come, God sent his Son, *born of a woman, born under law*' in order to redeem the people from the law. Similarly in Romans 1:3 - 4, he stated that 'Jesus Christ our Lord' was made 'of the seed of David *according to the flesh*' but 'was declared the son of God with power according to the spirit of holiness, by resurrection from the dead.'[56] The passage suggests not only that Jesus was a natural descendant of David, but also that his conception and birth were natural events, although he was later elevated to the status of the powerful Son of God by his subsequent resurrection from the dead. However, if Jesus had been naturally conceived and born, it would mean that he was not divine and therefore not an incarnation of God.[57] On the other hand, if he was fathered by the Holy Spirit as claimed in the gospel story, it would

---

[56] KJV (emphasis added).
[57] For a detailed discussion of the issue of divinity of Jesus, see Chapter 13.

mean that he had no Jewish bloodline, and therefore not the Messiah expected by the Jews. So, could Jesus have been the son of David as Apostle Paul claims?

CHAPTER 2

WAS JESUS THE SON OF DAVID?

Remember Jesus Christ, risen from the dead, descendant of David, according to my gospel. – 2 Timothy 2:8

The Hebrew Scriptures state that the Messiah expected by the Jews would be a descendant of David who would inherit the Davidic throne and kingdom. Accordingly, the gospels of Matthew and Luke assert that Jesus' name signified that he would be great, the Son of the most high, and inheritor of the throne of his father and ancestor – King David.[1] In addition, Matthew claims that the birth of Jesus was in fulfilment of the prophecy that out of Bethlehem would 'come a ruler who will be the shepherd of my people Israel'.[2] Several passages in the gospels also describe Jesus as 'the son of David'.[3]

However, the Bible makes it clear that Joseph, through whose bloodline Jesus' ancestry supposedly leads to David, was not the biological father of Jesus since he was the product of the Holy Spirit. Yet, elsewhere, the Bible appears to suggest that Joseph was a descendant of David, and that Jesus was a biological son of Joseph.

---

[1] See Luke 1: 30-33; Matthew 1; Luke 3:23-37
[2] See Matthew 2:1-6, and Micah 5:2.
[3] See e.g. Matthew 9: 27; Matthew 15: 22; Matthew 20: 30; Matthew 21: 15; Mark 10: 47.

For example, Matthew ended the genealogy linking Joseph to David by stating that Jacob was the father of Joseph, 'the husband of Mary, of whom was born Jesus, who is called Christ'. Luke, on his part, began his genealogy by stating that Jesus 'was the son, so it was thought, of Joseph, the son of Heli'.[4]

Therefore, on the one hand, the Holy Spirit rather than Joseph fathered Jesus; but on the other hand, he descended from David through Joseph. An explanation that Jesus became a descendant of David via his adoption by Joseph cannot overcome this contradiction. By 'descendant of David', the Bible clearly means somebody of the royal bloodline (or seed) of David – not anybody who might have been adopted – since Yahweh had apparently promised David and his blood descendants the kingship of Israel forever.[5] This being the case, a claim to the kingship of Israel would be baseless unless the claimant was from the bloodline of David.[6] Similarly, the genealogy of Jesus given in the gospels will be of no consequence if Joseph was not his biological father. Either Jesus was the son of David, or he was not. As the Oxford Dictionary of the Bible asks, 'If Jesus was provided miraculously with DNA, specially created by God, with no human

---

[4] See the next section of this chapter.
[5] See e.g. 2 Samuel 7: 15-16; Psalm 89; Amos 9: 11; Ezekiel 37: 24-27; John 7:42.
[6] There is no indication in the Bible that the lineage of Jesus was traced through the bloodline of his mother, Mary, contrary to the claim of the Christian Church, based largely on tradition (see e.g. 'The Genealogy of Christ', in the *Catholic Encyclopaedia*). Even if there were, such lineage would not count for much under Jewish law where lineage is traced through the father.

ancestry, how did he have a human inheritance of the house of David?'[7]

Moreover, the Bible claims that Jesus existed from the beginning of time and was co-equal and one with the Almighty God with whom he created all things.[8] If this were the case, it would follow that Jesus created David.[9] How then could Jesus have descended from David, his own creation? According to the Bible, Jesus asked the same question[10] before proceeding to cite Psalm 110:1 in refutation of the claim that he was the son of David who called him Lord.[11] That reference is, however, misplaced in that it assumed that David was the one speaking; and that King (Lord) David was addressing Lord Jesus when in fact the passage was 'a royal Psalm in which *a court official* cites promises of victory made to the Davidic King'.[12] A royal official was apparently speaking about the promises made to his Lord (the King) by THE LORD (Yahweh).[13]

---

[7] See WRF Browning, *Oxford Dictionary of the Bible* (Oxford University Press 2009) 372.

[8] See John 1:1-3.

[9] See John 8:58

[10] See Matthew 22:41-46.

[11] Psalm 11:1

[12] See The *New Oxford Annotated Bible, NRSV with the Apocrypha* (4th ed) (Oxford University Press 2010) 866.

[13] According to the Bible, 'the book of Psalms is an anthology, or more properly, an anthology of anthologies comprising several collections of hymns that were composed at various times and places in ancient Israel, mostly in the first half of the first millennium BCE. Although many are attributed to King David, and some to other individuals, scholars agree that few, if any, were actually written by them Rather, their authors, like those of many of the books in the Hebrew Bible, are anonymous'. (See the introductory notes to the Psalms (Date and Authorship) in *The New Oxford Annotated Bible,* ibid, 773.

In any case, the scriptures on the 'messianic' promises anticipate an earthly king who would physically assume the kingship of Israel in the manner of King David. Jesus, however, never ruled Israel and never delivered them from the dominion of foreign powers. Not only was he crucified by the Roman rulers of his time in the manner of criminals, the gospels report Jesus as pointedly repudiating any claims to Jewish or earthly kingship.[14] If Jesus Christ was not an earthly king,[15] if he never inherited the throne of David, and if he rejected any entitlement to that throne, it seems clear that he was not the fulfilment of any messianic prophecy made to the Jews. Moreover, Yahweh's purported promise that the royal dynasty of David and the whole kingdom of Israel would last forever and would be free from disturbance and oppression,[16] has failed to materialise. The Bible records that the house of David lost its hold on eighty per cent of the country shortly after the death of Solomon, David's son. The Northern Kingdom, comprising ten of the twelve tribes, went their own way with Jeroboam and formed an independent kingdom (Israel) with its capital in Samaria, leaving only two tribes – Judah and Benjamin (Judah) – to Rehoboam and David's subsequent descendants, apparently in accordance with divine will.[17] Thus, the same Yahweh who had promised the entire kingdom of Israel to the household of David forever, even in the face of transgression,[18] contrived to take

---

[14] See John 18:36.
[15] Except perhaps in connection with his anticipated second coming and millennium rule.
[16] See 2 Samuel 7:8 -16.
[17] See 1 Kings 12.
[18] See 2 Samuel 7:14-15.

most of it away from it soon after the death of David. Furthermore, the Northern Kingdom of Israel and the tribes comprising it were lost, following the conquest of Israel and the deportation, dispersion and assimilation of its people by the Assyrians around 721BC. The Babylonians did the same to the Southern Kingdom of Judah around 598 and 586 BCE, although they allowed many Judeans to return home later.[19] The Romans finally dispersed the returnees about 63 BC.[20] Given the foregoing, the claim in Luke's gospel about the kingship of Jesus over Israel could not be correct.

Was Jesus a Descendant of Adam?

The gospels did not end the ancestry of Jesus at David but traced it all the way to Abraham, Noah, Adam and God.[21] However, the genealogies as contained in Matthew and Luke are virtually meaningless; or, as the Catholic Encyclopaedia more kindly observes, contain many 'exegetical difficulties'.[22] The genealogy in Luke is different from the one in Matthew, in terms of not only the names and identity of his ancestors, but also of the number of generations that had passed before the birth of Jesus – 41 in Mathew and 77 in Luke.[23] Both records (especially Luke's) also contain many individuals unidentifiable in Hebrew history. According to the Biblical notes on Jesus' genealogy, 'the persons named from Heli (the father of Joseph)

---

[19] See https://www.britannica.com/topic/Ten-Lost-Tribes-of-Israel.
[20] See 2 Kings 25; WRF Browning, supra n 7, 164, 178.
[21] See Matthew 1: 1-17; Luke 3:23-38
[22] *The Catholic Encyclopaedia*, http://www.newadvent.org/cathen/06410a.htm.
[23] See J Barton and J Muddiman (eds.) *The Oxford Bible Commentary* (Oxford University Press 2007) 931.

to Zerubbabel are otherwise unknown'.[24] These non-existent characters represent nineteen generations in the genealogy. In addition, the ancestry of Jesus, according to Matthew, includes four non-Jewish women (Tamar, Rahab, Ruth and Bathsheba, the former wife of Uriah whom David had murdered) when, in fact, Jewish ancestry, as in all patriarchal societies, is traced only through male bloodlines.[25]

There is a suggestion that the names in the genealogies of Matthew and Luke are different because Matthew traced the genealogy through Joseph, while Luke traced it through Mary.[26] There is also a suggestion that the discrepancies as to the paternity of Joseph (Jacob was Joseph's father according to Matthew, but Heli was his father according to Luke) are reconcilable by the fact that the name of Joseph's father-in-law was Heli, entitling Joseph to the description 'son of Heli'.[27] These explanations are, however, futile as Jewish bloodlines and rights of inheritance run through fathers; not mothers or fathers-in-law. Moreover, these suggestions do not eliminate the discrepancies noted above.

These genealogies, especially Luke's, assume that the story of the creation of the world and the earliest human beings as related in the

---

[24] See also 1 Chronicles 3.
[25] See generally, the notes on Matthew 1:1-17 and Luke 3:23-38 in *The New Oxford Annotated Bible,* supra n 13, 1748, 1835; *The Catholic Encyclopaedia,* http://www.newadvent.org/cathen/06410a.htm. See also J Barton and J Muddiman, supra n 23, 848, 931; WRF Browning, supra n 7, 128.
[26] See e.g. www.theopedia.com.
[27] Ibid.

Bible are factually correct. However, it is self-evident that no human being can narrate the details of the process of creation that took place before anyone existed. Moreover, it is historically, archeologically and scientifically clear that the world did not begin in the Garden of Eden, and Adam and Eve were not the first human beings on earth.[28] The stories of the creation and the beginning of the universe, as narrated in the Bible book of Genesis, are mythical. They are similar to stories of different ancient peoples all over the world, especially those around the geographical location of the writers of Genesis, regarding how they imagined the world as they knew it came into being.[29]

Indeed, the name 'Adam' as used in the Bible was more a common name for a human being (man and woman) than a personal name for an individual,[30] or simply the Hebrew word for 'man.' *Adam* is also similar to *Adamah*, the Hebrew word for ground.[31] That Adam and his family were not the first or only human beings in existence even in the

---

[28] J Barton and J Muddiman (eds.) supra n 23, 42, 48.

[29] See e.g., W Rex, *Encyclopaedia of World Mythology* (London: BPC Limited London 1975) 13; P Wilkinson and N Phillip, *Mythology* (London: Doring Kindersley Ltd 2007) 18-19, 22-26, 36-37; A Cotterell, *The Illustrated Encyclopaedia of Myths and Legends* (Marshall editions Ltd 1989) 27, 113, 174. See further, D Rosenberg, *World Mythology: An Anthology of the Great Myths and Epics* (McGraw Hill Companies Inc. 1994); S Price and E Kearns, *The Oxford Dictionary of Classical Myth and Religion* (Oxford University Press 2003) 5, 75. See also *The New Oxford Annotated Bible*, supra n 12, 19; *Encyclopaedia Britannica*, http://www.britannica.com/topic/creation-myth; J Barton and J Muddiman (eds.) supra n 23, 40-46.

[30] See Genesis 1:26 – 31; and Genesis 5: 1 – 2.

[31] See annotations to Genesis 2:7; 4:1-18; 5:2 in *The New Oxford Annotated Bible*, supra n 12. See also WRF Browning (ed.) supra n 7, 4.

area near the 'Garden of Eden' is illustrated by the story of Cain and Abel; the punishment given to Cain for murdering Abel; Cain's sojourn and marriage in the land of Nod (which means 'wanderer'); and the marriage of Seth.[32] If Adam's was the first and only human family at the time, there would have been no need to fear that other people might kill Cain; and there would have been no wife for Cain and Seth to marry. Further illustrating the absurdity of the story is the suggestion that a couple supposed to fill the earth with their children[33] were not aware of their nakedness, and only discovered that fact after eating the 'forbidden' fruit. One also has to wonder how a snake spoke to Eve when snakes do not speak; and whether the 'Tree of Life' is still in the Garden under the guard of Cherubim and flaming swords. If the creation stories and the characters mentioned in them are not factual, it cannot be factual that Jesus descended from Noah and Adam. The principal Hebrew ancestors – Abraham, Isaac and Jacob – who are part of Jesus' family tree appear equally to be mythical characters in Jewish folklore.[34] The conclusion is therefore inescapable: The genealogies arose from a desire by the gospel writers to depict Jesus as the second Adam,[35] just as the story of his conception and birth appears to reflect common religious mythology.

---

[32] See Genesis 4:1-18.

[33] See Genesis 1:28.

[34] See http://www.jewishencyclopedia.com/articles/360-abraham.

[35] J Barton and J Muddiman (eds.) supra n 23, 843, 931.

CHAPTER 3

DIVINE CONCEPTIONS IN RELIGION AND FOLKLORE

The myth of Osiris shows some analogies with the Gospel story and, in the figure of Isis, with the role of the Virgin Mary. - Encyclopedia Britannica

Myths and legends abound in many religions and cultures, including those much more ancient than Christianity. Many of these myths centre on divine conceptions of god-men and their birth by virgin mothers.[1] Ancient Egyptians, who exerted arguably the greatest influence on the life and culture of ancient Israelites, believed that the god Horus was born by the virgin godmother, Isis.[2] Adherents of the

---

[1] See generally, *The Myth Encyclopaedia*, http://www.mythencyclopedia.com/Go-Hi/Heroes.html. Regarding the legend of Virgin Mary, see A Cotterell, *The Illustrated Encyclopaedia of Myths and Legends* (Marshall editions Ltd 1989) 27, 113, 174. For the Horus-Isis legend, see DM Murdock, *Christ in Egypt: the Horus-Jesus Connection* (Steller house Publishing 2009) 120-138. See also GF Chesnut, *Images of Christ: An Introduction to Christology* (Seabury Press 1984), 89.

[2] See Chapter 13 and A Cotterell, supra n 1, 65-66, 80, 105-106, 108-109. See also generally, P Wilkinson and N Phillip, *Mythology* (London: Doring Kindersley Ltd 2007) 286-291; JG Frazer, *Adonis Attis Osiris: Studies in the History of Oriental Religion* (London: Macmillan and Co. Ltd. 1906).

ancient Persian religion of Zoroastrianism[3] believe that their messiah, Saoshyant, was conceived and born by a virgin after she was exposed to the miraculously preserved seed of Zoroaster in a lake.[4] Saoshyant, in the eschatology of Zoroastrianism, is the final Saviour of the world and the foremost of three Saviours[5], all of whom would be products of posthumous conception from the miraculously preserved seed of Zoroaster – the founder of the religion.[6] In the tradition of Mithraism, another ancient religion, which was related to Zoroastrianism and widespread in the Roman Empire until supplanted by Christianity in the 5th century, Mithra was miraculously born from a rock.[7] Like Jesus, shepherds adored him, and he had rituals, including baptism and Eucharist.[8] Moreover, like Jesus, he was supposedly the mediator between humans and God, and saved the world by sacrificing a bull.[9] Before Christianity, the faithful celebrated Mithra's birthday on 25 December. According to the Oxford Dictionary of the Bible, 'the

---

[3] The religion dates to as far back as 3500 BCE and is still practised around the world, albeit in small numbers. See http://www.worldatlas.com/articles/top-countries-of-the-world-by-zoroastrian-population.html.

[4] See *The Encyclopaedia Britannica,* http://www.britannica.com/EBchecked/topic/523625/Saoshyans; see also *The Catholic encyclopaedia,* http://www.newadvent.org/cathen/02154a.htm.

[5] Others are Oshetar and Oshetarmah.

[6] On this, see further A Cotterell, Supra n 1, 75, 156. See also S Archaya, *The Christ Conspiracy: The Greatest Story Ever Sold* (Adventures Unlimited Press 2012) 122-124.

[7] See J Bowker (ed) *Oxford Dictionary of World Religions* (Oxford University Press 1997).

[8] R Goring (ed) Larouse Dictionary of Beliefs and Religions (Kingfisher Publications PLC; New Edition 1994).

[9] See *The Catholic Encyclopaedia,* http://www.newadvent.org/cathen/10402a.htm, 27 May 2015. See also D Crystal (ed.) supra n 104, 1016.

Mithraic festival of the *Natalis Solis invicti* on 25 December was taken over as Christmas Day by the Church in the 4th cent.'[10]

Concerning the birth of Gautama Buddha, the founder of Buddhism, legend has it that his mother (Queen Maya) had a dream in which four angels carried her to a mountaintop, where they clothed her with flowers. Then a white bull elephant came to her, carrying a white lotus flower in its trunk. The elephant walked round Maya three times, struck her by the side and disappeared into her. The wise men of the land interpreted the dream as meaning that the queen would bear a son, and if the son stayed in the palace, he would be a great man; but if he left, he would be a Buddha. When childbirth approached, Maya travelled from the king's capital to the town of her own birth. On the way to the place, Queen Maya came across a grove with blossoming flowers. When she reached out to touch the flowers, she gave birth. The child stood up, took seven steps and said, 'I alone am the world-honoured one'. Maya died after seven days, leaving the child – Buddha – in the care of her sister, who was also married to the king.[11] Thus, Buddha, like Jesus, was the product of an asexual conception, and manifested super-natural qualities immediately after he was born – being able to stand and speak instantly.

---

[10] See S Archaya, supra n 6, 118-120; J Frazer, supra n 2, 195-202; P Wilkinson and N Phillip, supra n 2, 95.

[11] See J Bowker (ed) supra n 7. See also the *Encyclopaedia Britannica*, http://www.britannica.com/EBchecked/topic/323556/Krishna; S Archaya, supra n 6, 108-111.

In Hinduism, devotees believe that Krishna was the eighth avatar or incarnation of Vishnu, one of the deities in the Hindu trinity (others being Brahma and Shiva). He was the eighth child of his mother, Devaki. On the birth of Krishna, the reigning wicked king of Mathura, Kamsa – the brother of Devaki – sought to kill him. This was because of a prophecy from a heavenly voice that the eighth child of Devaki would kill Kamsa. Following this prophecy, Kamsa imprisoned Devaki and her husband, and proceeded to kill the first seven children of Devaki. When Krishna was born in the prison, Kamsa plotted to kill him. However, this plot fell through when, with divine intervention and guidance, Krishna was smuggled out of the prison into the care of foster parents. When he grew up, Krishna killed Kamsa and liberated the people of Mathura from his tyrannical government.[12] Thus, like Jesus, Krishna was supposedly the incarnation of the Supreme God. Like Jesus, his birth apparently followed a divine prophecy; and like Jesus, a jealous and wicked king unsuccessfully sought to destroy him at infancy in order to prevent his destiny and mission from being realised. Krishna was also a messiah who had come to deliver his people from oppression. Hindus also revere Rama as the incarnation of Vishnu. He was the seventh Avatar, and with Krishna, are the most widely worshipped Hindu deities.[13]

---

[12] See J Bowker (ed.) supra n 7. See also *the Encyclopaedia Britannica*, http://www.britannica.com/EBchecked/topic/323556/Krishna.
[13] See *the Catholic Encyclopaedia*, http://www.newadvent.org/cathen/02730a.htm. See also Archaya S, supra n 6, 116-118.

In Aztec mythology, the god Huitzilopochtli was allegedly conceived when his goddess-mother stuffed hummingbird feathers into her chest. He subsequently emerged from his mother's womb a fully-grown person.[14] Other religious heroes allegedly having a divine conception include, *Kutoyis*, the hero of the Native American Blackfoot people, who was born as a clot of blood dropped by a buffalo; and *Kama*, the Mahabharata hero who was allegedly born by a virgin.[15] Legend also has it that Roman founders Romulus and Remus were the asexual products of a virgin.[16] These examples show that the biblical stories about the nativity of Jesus are neither peculiar, nor much different from the legends of other religions. These tales appear to be attempts to clothe religious beliefs with the garb of reality.[17] As explained by the Oxford Dictionary of World Religions,[18] the widespread claims of virgin birth in many religions 'is a reverential theme introduced for apologetic reasons'.[19]

---

[14] See the Myths Encyclopaedia, http://www.mythencyclopedia.com/Ho-Iv/Huitzilopochtli.html.

[15] See *The Myth Encyclopaedia,* http://www.mythencyclopedia.com/Go-Hi/Heroes.html.

[16] See *The Myth Encyclopaedia,* http://www.mythencyclopedia.com/Pr-Sa/Romulus-and-Remus.html.

[17] See, WRF Browning, *Oxford Dictionary of the Bible* (Oxford University Press 2009) 160 for a summation of the purport of the Bible stories. See generally, U Ranke-Heinemann, *Putting away Childish Things: The Virgin Birth, the Empty Tomb, Hell and Other Fairy Tales You Don't Need to Believe to Have a Living Faith* (Harper San Francisco 1994)

[18] J Bowker (ed) supra n 7, 1025 – 1026.

[19] For a more detailed examination of the subject, see JG Frazer, *Adonis Attis Osiris: Studies in the History of Oriental Religion* (London: Macmillan and Co. Ltd. 1906), 3-8, 163-175; 211-219; D Rosenberg, *World Mythology: An Anthology of the Great Myths and Epics* (McGraw Hill Companies Inc. 1994), 160-162. See

Are we entitled to reject these competing stories as myth and accept the story of the conception and birth of Jesus as real when it has no historical attestation? It is not surprising that some of the earliest Christian authorities and sects, including church fathers and bishops, never believed in a physical Jesus, perceiving his existence in an entirely spiritual and cosmic sense. It took several Ecumenical Councils centuries after the beginning of Christianity to establish the orthodox doctrine of the incarnation of a human Jesus who is part of the Holy Trinity, and of the same substance as God the Father.[20] Following this, the church proscribed as heresies all 'unorthodox' doctrines and excommunicated their advocates. Nevertheless, Nontrinitarian Christian denominations, to this day, still reject the orthodox position.[21] The mythical complexion of the Nativity, like that of pre-existing religions, forms the basis of the celebration of Christmas in mainstream Christianity.

Christmas and the Birth of Gods

Although most Christians celebrate December 25 as the day of Christmas (*Cristes Maesse* or Mass of Christ), Jesus was clearly not born on that day. The accounts of his birth in the Bible do not specify the day, month or year of birth,[22] and the early Christians did not

---

also S Archaya, supra n 6, 107-125; S Price and E Kearns, *The Oxford Dictionary of Classical Myth and Religion* (Oxford University Press 2003) 5, 75.

[20] For a detailed discussion of this, see Chapter 13.

[21] For a discussion of this, see Chapter 13.

[22] The claim in Luke's gospel about angels appearing to shepherds who were watching over their flock at night has been dismissed by all in the know as implausible since flocks and shepherds do not stay out in the fields through the night in winter. The 'worldwide census' which Luke claimed to have taken place around the time of Jesus' birth, and which required everybody to travel to their ancestral

celebrate the birth of Jesus on December 25 or any other day. Since Christians began to celebrate Jesus' birthday many centuries after the advent of the religion, the church has – at different periods – assigned the birthday to several different months in the year.[23] It was not until after 400 CE[24] that Christendom settled on December 25 as the birthday of Jesus. However, it is incontrovertible that the church adopted that date to coincide with the Winter Solstice and the pre-existing festival of *Sol Invictus*[25] (Unconquered Sun), celebrated in Roman 'pagan' religions in honour of the sun god.[26] In the words of the Catholic Encyclopaedia, 'the well-known solar feast [...] of *Natalis Invicti*, celebrated on 25 December, has a strong claim on the responsibility for our December date.'[27]

The display of 'Christmas' trees and plant wreaths at Christmas is of relatively recent origin, and has nothing to do with the birth of Jesus. It is a tradition traceable to the customs of ancient peoples around the world (including Africans, the Chinese, the Hebrews and the Europeans) who regarded trees and plants as symbols of life, and venerated them accordingly. This tradition among Europeans is most significant because the modern custom concerning Christmas trees

---

homes was also implausible in winter. See *The Catholic Encyclopaedia*, http://www.newadvent.org/cathen/03724b.htm.

[23] See *The Catholic Encyclopaedia*,
http://www.newadvent.org/cathen/03724b.htm.

[24] That is more than four hundred years after the supposed death of Jesus.

[25] Alternatively, *Natalis Invicti*.

[26] See WRF Browning, supra n 17, 56; *The Catholic Encyclopaedia*,
http://www.newadvent.org/cathen/03724b.htm. Rather than being holy, the festival was marked by wanton revelry, drunkenness and debauchery.

[27] See http://www.newadvent.org/cathen/02084a.htm.

and wreaths originated in Europe, where it was common to decorate homes with evergreen trees for different reasons during the midwinter holidays.[28] The association of Christmas trees with Christmas is particularly traceable to Germany, where people often placed in their homes a 'Paradise Tree' (a fir tree laden with apples) and the 'Christmas Pyramid' to mark the religious feast of Adam and Eve that was held on December 24. The practice subsequently reached the USA and the rest of the world between the 17th and 20th centuries through German and other Western migrants, many of whom were Christian missionaries.[29]

Santa Claus, (or Father Christmas) who supposedly comes from the North Pole on reindeer-drawn sleighs to distribute gifts to children, has no association with the birth of Jesus. Instead, he originated from Holland in commemoration of the feast of Saint Nicholas, a legendary 4th century Christian saint. From the Dutch, who held the feast of St Nicholas on December 6, the legend of Santa Claus got to New York and the rest of the world.[30] However, the current popular configuration of Santa Claus derives from a 19th century cartoon made popular by a Coca Cola advertisement in early 1930s.[31] Other traditions and

---

[28] See *The Encyclopaedia Britannica*,
http://www.britannica.com/EBchecked/topic/115737/Christmas-tree.
[29] Ibid.
See also *The Catholic Encyclopaedia*,
http://www.newadvent.org/cathen/03724b.htm.
[30] See the *Catholic Encyclopaedia*, http://www.newadvent.org/cathen/11063b.htm.
[31] See *The Encyclopaedia Britannica*,
http://www.britannica.com/EBchecked/topic/522799/Santa-Claus.

imagery associated with Christmas, such as door wreaths and reindeers, also have no bearing on the birth of Jesus.[32]

Does it matter that Christians celebrate Jesus' birth on a day he was certainly not born? Yes, it does. If the birth had actually happened, as narrated in the Bible (even though one would still have to choose between Matthew and Luke's account), the day and month of its occurrence would have stuck in traditional Christian consciousness. The church would therefore not need to copy a pre-existing 'pagan' festival. The exceptional conception and the miraculous circumstances surrounding the birth and early life of Jesus could not but be engraved in the memories of his parents, siblings,[33] townspeople, and others who witnessed or heard of them. These would include Elizabeth – the mother of John the Baptist – to whom Mary went after the conception, causing the child in her womb to leap with joy;[34] and Simeon – the priest who consecrated the baby Jesus and recognised him as the messiah.[34] Given the Bible's claim that Jesus' mother, siblings, disciples and numerous followers witnessed his ministry, crucifixion, resurrection and ascension, and outlived him, it is implausible that they would not remember when he was born, unless they all suffered from acute and chronic amnesia or dementia.

---

[32] See e.g. David Crystal (ed.) *The Penguin Encyclopaedia* (Penguin Books 2004) 325.
[33] See Matthew 13:55; Mark 6:3.
[34] See Luke 2:25-35.

Furthermore, it is a known fact that many early Christians did not believe in the physical birth, death and resurrection of Jesus. Indeed, the 'heretical' belief in a non-human Jesus, known as Docetism, had quickly gained substantial ground among believers. This belief prompted the writer of the epistles of John to condemn the propagators as the 'antichrist'.[35] This situation might have influenced the inauguration of the birthday of Jesus as a way of re-affirming his human and material reality among Christians, especially since his second coming – which his followers fully expected to happen in their lifetime – failed to materialise. However, the selection of December 25 to mark the birthday of Jesus identifies him with the sun gods of so-called pagan religions whose supposed births worshippers celebrate on the same day. It was apparently for this reason that the English Parliament outlawed Christmas in 1644 as immoral and unchristian.[36] It is also for that reason that many Christian denominations, including the Jehovah's Witnesses, the Restored Church of God, and the Christian Churches of God, do not celebrate Christmas but expressly condemn it.[37] Since the tales of the conception and birth of Jesus lack veracity and substance, would those

---

[35] See 1 John 4:1-3; 2 John 7. See also *Encyclopaedia Britannica,*
http://www.britannica.com/topic/Docetism; *The Oxford Dictionary of the Bible,*
supra n 32, 56.

[36] The law was only abolished in 1660 when Oliver Cromwell, whose government masterminded the legislation, died and the monarchy was restored.

[37] For the position of the Jehovah's Witnesses, see http://www.jw.org/en/bible-teachings/questions/bible-about-christmas/; for the position of the Restored Church of God, see http://rcg.org/search.html?q=christmas; and for the position of the Christian Churches of God, see http://www.ccg.org/c/cb024.htmlm.

of his adult life – beginning from his baptism and temptation – be different?

CHAPTER 4

WAS JESUS BAPTISED BY JOHN?

Baptism is not merely for the purpose of expiating a special transgression, as is the case chiefly in the violation of the so-called Levitical laws of purity; but it is to form a part of holy living and to prepare for the attainment of a closer communion with God. – Jewish Encyclopaedia[1]

The first recorded activity of Jesus' adult life in the Bible was his baptism by John the Baptist – an event that apparently invested him and his ministry with divine endorsement, and gave rise to the sacrament of baptism in Christianity. Baptism by immersion in, or sprinkling of, water is a common but important ritual in certain religions, not in the least Judaism and Christianity, where it is commonly a pre-condition for admission into the faith. According to the Jewish Encyclopaedia, baptism is a 'religious ablution signifying purification or consecration. The natural method of cleansing the body by washing and bathing in water was always customary in Israel.'[2]

Some mystery religions and occult societies also perform baptism or other initiation rites on believers and new intakes, with water, blood or fire. The essence of baptism or initiation rituals is to cleanse and

---

[1] http://www.jewishencyclopedia.com/articles/2456-baptism.
[2] Ibid.

make worthy of admission into a faith or society, indicating in the novice a prior state of uncleanness and unworthiness. Accordingly, the Jewish Encyclopaedia explains that baptism is required in order to 'form a part of holy living and to prepare for the attainment of a closer communion with God.'[3] The ritual washing or cleaning of parts of the body as a way of purification performed in Judaism and Islam is similar to baptism. However, the question arises as to whether Jesus was baptised; and if so, why. Another question is whether human beings need to be baptised or ritually cleansed in order to be acceptable to God.

The Gospel Story

The synoptic gospels report that John the Baptist, the putative forerunner, baptised Jesus before he commenced his ministry. In fact, the Gospel of Mark begins with the story of the baptism.[4] According to the narrative, John the Baptist was 'baptising in the desert region and preaching a baptism of repentance for the forgiveness of sins', and people from the Judean countryside and Jerusalem went to him, confessing their sins and getting baptised in the River Jordan. In the course of his ministrations, John declared that a more powerful person than he would appear, the laces of whose shoes he would not be worthy to untie.[5] The forthcoming person would not baptise with water, as John did, but with the Holy Spirit. Jesus then came forward to John in the River Jordan, and was baptised. As Jesus left the river,

---

[3] Ibid.
[4] Mark 1: 1 – 3.
[5] Mark 1: 4 – 8.

the heaven was 'torn open' and 'the Spirit' in the form of a dove descended on him, and a voice proclaimed from heaven: 'You are my Son, whom I love; with you I am well pleased.'[6] The accounts of Matthew[7] and Luke[8] are similar to Mark's, except that in Matthew John initially protested that he was the one who should be baptised by Jesus, but later relented and baptised Jesus in order to 'fulfil all righteousness'.

According to the synoptic gospels, the baptism by John, and the imminent ministry of Jesus, were in fulfilment of the prophecy in Isaiah 40:3: 'A voice of one calling: "In the desert prepare the way for the LORD; make straight in the wilderness a highway for our God."' In addition, the baptism apparently confirmed Jesus as the divine Son of God, especially by the physical landing of the Holy Spirit upon him, and the approving declaration from heaven by God. The baptism also readied Jesus for his earthly ministry, since he was thereafter able to overcome the determined temptations of the devil and commence his ministry.[9] Apparently following the example of Jesus, the Christian church instituted baptism as a means of admittance into the 'body of Christ'. It is unlikely, however, that the baptism ever took place.

Contrary to the synoptic accounts, John's gospel reports that Jesus was not baptised by John the Baptist or anybody else. Instead, John the Baptist gave a private testimony to his listeners about Jesus who

---

[6] Mark 1: 9 – 11.
[7] Matthew 3.
[8] Luke 3.
[9] See Chapters 5 and 6.

happened to be coming towards them. He informed them that Jesus was the Lamb of God that would take away the sins of the world and baptise people with the Holy Spirit, and that he – John – was his forerunner. Observing that he did not know Jesus before that time, the Baptist testified that he saw the Spirit in the form of a dove descend and stay on him. Following an earlier tip off by God that, 'He on whom you see the Spirit descend and remain is the one who baptises with the Holy Spirit', John testified that Jesus was the son of God.[10] Thus, not only did John not baptise Jesus; the descent of the dove on Jesus was a private event observed only by the Baptist. There was no opening of the heavens, or a voice declaring loudly that Jesus was God's beloved and pleasing son. The synoptic and John's gospels therefore contradict each other on whether or not John baptised Jesus.

Further undermining the credibility of the baptism narrative is the fact that John the Baptist did not appear to know who Jesus was, before and after the baptism. As noted above, John appeared to have met Jesus for the first time just before the baptism. How could John not have known Jesus when both were supposedly close and miraculously conceived cousins whose births the Angel Gabriel forecast? Remember that John's mother – Elizabeth – had recognised that Mary was pregnant with the Saviour.[11] One would reasonably expect that, in these circumstances, John and Jesus would know each other reasonably well as they grew up. Another question is how John – who

---

[10] John 1: 19 – 34.
[11] See Luke 1:39-45.

had been preparing 'the way of the Lord' – did not know 'the Lord' despite all the wonders surrounding Jesus' conception, birth and early life. Even more significant is the fact that John did not appear to know that Jesus was the Messiah even after the baptism. When he was in prison, and having heard of his exploits, John had sent messengers to Jesus, asking: 'Are you the Coming One, or do we look for another?' To convince John that he was the One, Jesus referred the messengers to the miracles, signs and wonders he was performing.[12] How could John ask this question when he was Jesus' forerunner? How could he pose such a question when he heard and saw the heavens confirm Jesus' status at his baptism, and had declared Jesus the Lamb of God that would take away the sins of the world?

In addition, the claim that the baptism fulfilled Old Testament prophesies is not correct. The prophecy of Isaiah 40:3 referred to above was not in any way concerned with the baptism or ministry of Jesus. Rather, it was 'a renewed prophetic commission to announce the Lord's restoration of Zion […] and announces that the time of the restoration is at hand'.[13] It thus concerned the revival of Israel following the long period of exile in Babylon, after King Cyrus of Persia had conquered Babylon and decreed that the Jews could return home between 545 and 539 BC. All the above suggest that the baptism narrative is far from credible. Nevertheless, if Jesus were indeed

---

[12] See Luke 7:18-22.

[13] The note on Isaiah 40:3 in *New Oxford Annotated Bible, NRSV with the Apocrypha* (4th ed) (Oxford University Press 2010) 1019-1020.

.

baptised as the synoptic gospels claim, what would be its significance to the claim that he is the Saviour of the world?

Significance of Baptism

As reported in the Bible,[14] John the Baptist preached 'a baptism of repentance for the forgiveness of sins', and the people went to him to confess their sins and be baptised. Jesus apparently went to John for that purpose, given that after the event, heaven gave him and his incipient ministry its seal of approval. This understanding is consistent with Jewish practice where baptism was customary for penitence, purification and consecration. As the Jewish Encyclopaedia points out, 'baptism is not merely for the purpose of expiating a special transgression, as is the case chiefly in the violation of the so-called Levitical laws of purity; but it is to form a part of holy living, and to prepare for the attainment of a closer communion with God.'[15] Thus, baptism or immersion for the purpose of cleansing and purification is essential for new priests, women after childbirth, converts to Judaism, the dead before burial, men during the Yom Kippur (Day of Atonement), among others.[16]

This begs the question why Jesus needed to be baptised by the Baptist when he was supposed to be God incarnate. Matthew's gospel attempted to explain this embarrassing conundrum by claiming that

---

[14] See Mark 1:4-5.
[15] See the *Jewish Encyclopaedia*,
http://www.jewishencyclopedia.com/articles/2456-baptism.
[16] Some have in fact claimed that Jesus' baptism took place on the Day of Atonement. For this, see for example,
http://www.theopenscroll.com/beyond_veil/appendices/baptism.htm.

the baptism was in order to 'fulfil all righteousness' in the sense that it was merely a symbolic activity. This claim seems lame and illogical, since – as noted above – Jesus did not begin his ministry until after his baptism, and it was only after it that he gained endorsement as the Son of God. In effect, the baptism validated Jesus' ministry and relationship with God, meaning that it was not merely symbolic. The baptism could therefore only have been with a view to repentance, purification and forgiveness of sins. In defence, the Catholic Church has presented some rationalisation for Jesus' baptism.[17]

First, it argues that Jesus chose to be baptised not because he needed cleansing but in order to cleanse and sanctify the water for the benefit of other baptism candidates. This claim, however, lacks merit, presupposing as it were, that the River Jordan had been unclean all along. This could not have been true since John had been using the same river for his baptism and had baptised many people therein before Jesus came along.[18] The claim is also speculative as neither Jesus nor John said or implied so, and flies in the face of traditional Jewish belief that, the waters of the River Jordan 'restore the unclean man to the original state of a new-born 'little child'.[19] Moreover, the claim that Jesus had no sin for which he would need cleansing is

---

[17] See the *Catholic Encyclopaedia,* http://www.newadvent.org/summa/4039.htm.
[18] Mark 1: 5; Matthew 3: 4 – 5; Luke 3: 21.
[19] See the *Jewish Encyclopaedia,*
http://www.jewishencyclopedia.com/articles/2456-baptism.

unsupported by evidence, as there are no details of his private life in the Bible.[20]

Second, the church states that Jesus, having been born in the flesh, and become tainted with the 'Original Sin' of Adam, was baptised in order to banish that sinful nature in the waters. This justification is fallacious since it assumes the veracity of the creation myth in Genesis and the legitimacy of the church's dogma of 'Original Sin', which lack merit.[21] It also ignores the fact that John's baptism did not target any inherent sinful nature but only committed sins. In any event, since the Bible describes Jesus as God incarnate born through Holy Spirit conception, he could not have inherited the supposed sinful nature of Adam.

Third, the church asserts that by going through a baptism he did not need, Jesus set an example to his followers and others. However, the baptism of John, as already observed, was not a token gesture but expressly stated to be an instrument for penance and the forgiveness of sins. This is in conformity with Jewish and Christian practices where baptism also doubles as a requirement for admission into the assembly of believers. In the church dogma, the sacrament of baptism is the door to spiritual life and into the body of Christ, and cleanses people from sin without which they could not enter the kingdom of God.[22] This dogma reflects the teaching of Jesus that, 'no one can

---

[20] See Chapter 11.
[21] See LE Modeme, *Fantasy of Salvation* (Ameze Resources Ltd. 2019).
[22] See *Roman Catholic Catechism 1213*, http://www.vatican.va/archive/ENG0015/__P3G.HTM; The *Anglican Catechism,*

enter the kingdom of God unless he is born of water and the Spirit.'[23] Consequently, he reportedly enjoined his disciples to 'go and make disciples of all nations, baptizing them in the name of the Father and of the Son and of the Holy Spirit'.[24] Those who believe and are baptised will be saved, 'but whoever does not believe will be condemned'.[25]

Other forms of Ritual Cleansing

Akin to baptism are the various rites of purification for ridding people of supposed ritual uncleanliness and making them fit to be in the presence of God. In Judaism, for example, persons cured of leprosy and other 'defiling' skin diseases must undergo ritual cleansing before they would be purified. The cleansing involves the offer of sacrifice, washing of clothes and body, and shaving of beards and hair.[26] Men who have body or semen discharge, including during sexual intercourse, would also be unclean. To return to cleanliness, they and anyone they touch must – in addition to making sin and burnt offerings – ritually wash their clothes and body in water.[27] In like manner after menstruation and any irregular discharge of blood, women, and anything or anyone they touch, would also be unclean. To render themselves clean again, the parties must ritually wash their clothes

---

http://anglicansonline.org/basics/catechism.html#Holy Baptism. See also *The Catholic Encyclopaedia*, http://www.newadvent.org/cathen/02258b.htm.
[23] John 3: 5.
[24] Matthew 28: 19. See also Romans 6: 3-4, Colossians 2:11-12.
[25] Mark 16: 15-16. See also John 3: 4-5.
[26] Leviticus 14:1-32.
[27] Leviticus 15:1-18.

and body in water.[28] In addition to washing the body, ritual washing of clothes is also important for purification and consecration.[29] The Mosaic Law requires that anyone who ate an animal that died naturally, or which was killed by a wild animal, must ritually wash their clothes and body in order to regain cleanliness.[30] On the Day of Atonement, the priest must remove his clothes and wash his entire body in the holy place before performing sacrifice. Likewise, the men that release the scapegoat or burn the sacrificial animal must also wash their bodies before re-entering the camp.[31]

Similar to the Mosaic Law, the Quran[32] enjoins Moslems to perform ritual washing and cleaning – *wudu* and *ghusl* – at certain times. The former refers to the washing of the face and hands (up to the elbows), while the latter refers to the wiping of the head and feet (up to the ankles). These cleansings must be done with pure and ritually clean water and should be accompanied by the recitation of certain prayers. *Wudu* is mandatory during obligatory prayers, compulsory circumambulation, touching the writings of the Quran, touching the names and attributes of Allah, and after making a promise or vow to be in a state of ritual cleanliness.[33] Stooling, farting, discharge of urine and semen, menstruation, irregular and post-natal bleeding,

---

[28] Leviticus 15:19-30.
[29] Exodus 19:10.
[30] Leviticus 17:15-16.
[31] Leviticus 16; Numbers 19:19.
[32] Surah 5:6.
[33] https://www.al-islam.org/ritual-and-spiritual-purity-sayyid-muhammad-rizvi/ii-wudu.

drunkenness, sound sleep, unconsciousness and insanity could invalidate ritual cleanliness.[34]

It is obligatory for Moslems to perform *ghusl* in situations of some *Janabat* or defilement. These are sexual intercourse, any discharge of semen or seminal fluid by men, and any discharge by women of sexual fluid in a state of passion. A person rendered unclean in the above circumstances is forbidden from entering or staying in a mosque, touching the Quran or mentioning the names and attributes of Allah. They must also not mention the name of the prophet, recite verses of the Quran requiring prostration, or leave in or take something from a mosque.[35] Nevertheless, while baptism and ritual cleansing might be essential practices in the Jewish, Christian and Islamic faiths, are they necessary really for communion with or closeness to God?

Is Baptism and Ritual Cleansing the Way to God?

Although it might have ritualistic and fellowship significance, it is unlikely that baptism has any effect in cleansing people from wrongdoing. A murderer would not suddenly become free of guilt or the blood of his victim because he or she has been baptised into the assembly of believers. Conversely, a guiltless person would not become unclean or excluded from divine presence or favour simply because he or she has not been baptised into a particular religious faith. In addition, where – as in many Christian denominations – baptisms are performed on infants who cannot be unclean, and who

---

[34] Ibid.
[35] Ibid.

have no idea what they are undergoing, it is difficult to see how such a ritual would or should affect the person's destiny.

Similarly, the performance of rituals or physical shows of cleanliness might not be necessary for the admittance of people into the presence or kingdom of God. Ablutions, circumcision, long beards, long hair, head and face coverings, and similar outward shows of belongingness, piety or cleansing, might be necessary for initiation into, and identification with, religions and societies, but they are not necessary for identification or connection with God. This is because humans have an innate and natural connection to God. Evidently, a person baptised and adjudged clean and worthy of God in one religious faith would not be clean or acceptable in other religions by virtue of that baptism. That Jesus felt the need to be baptised suggests that he could only have been a human being fulfilling the rituals of his people, assuming of course, that he existed and the baptism in fact occurred.

CHAPTER 5

WAS JESUS TEMPTED BY THE DEVIL?

Immediately the Spirit drove him into the wilderness. And He was there in the wilderness forty days, tempted by Satan, and was with the wild beasts; and the angels ministered to him. - Mark 1: 12-13

S tories of religious heroes overcoming temptations at the beginning, or in the course of their lives or ministries, are common. Such stories depict the extraordinary character and grace of the persons concerned, as well as their ability to withstand temptations where mere mortals would have failed. They also attempt to show the victory of a 'Man of God' over the machinations of the devil. These appear to be the case with the story of Jesus' temptation.

The Story of Jesus' Temptation

The gospels of Matthew and Luke[1] report Jesus as facing three temptations immediately after he was baptised and before he commenced his ministry. The temptation accounts in Matthew[2] and

---

[1] Mark merely alludes to Jesus being led into the wilderness by the spirit and being tempted by the devil, and being attended by the angels. He provided no details. See Mark 1: 12-13. John makes no references to Jesus being led into the wilderness or his being tempted by the devil.

[2] See Matthew 4:1-11.

Luke[3] are virtually identical, except in the order of the second and third temptations. In the accounts, after his baptism, Jesus was immediately led 'by the spirit' into the desert 'to be tempted of the devil'. He was in the desert for forty days and nights during which time he ate nothing. It is not clear whether he drank anything; but since he was alone in the desert and since he appeared to take no provisions, he – presumably – drank nothing as well. At the end of the fast, Jesus was understandably hungry. At this point, the devil appeared. The devil's first temptation was to ask Jesus to turn stone into bread if he were truly the son of God. Jesus rebuffed the devil by reminding him that man must not live by food alone but by the word of God. Next, the devil took Jesus to a high mountain and from there showed him 'all the kingdoms of the world' and promised to give them all to him if Jesus bowed down and worshipped him. Jesus promptly rebuked the devil by informing him that only God deserves worship and service.

Finally, the devil took Jesus to Jerusalem and to the pinnacle of the city's temple. He asked Jesus to prove that he was the son of God by throwing himself down from that height since it was written that God, 'will command his angels concerning you, and they will lift you up in their hands, so that you will not strike your foot against a stone'. To this latest temptation, Jesus answered that, 'it is also written: "Do not put the Lord your God to the test."' After this, and having failed in his

---

[3] See Luke 4:1-13.

nefarious endeavours, the devil left Jesus, to whom angels of God came to attend.

The temptation story has great significance to the ministry of Jesus. Having just been baptised by John the Baptist and having received confirmation as God's beloved and pleasing son, his readiness to start his ministry and withstand temptation went on test. Presumably, if Jesus had failed the devil's test, he would not have been able to commence his ministry, at least at that point. As it turned out, he appeared to pass with flying colours. However, did Jesus really pass any test?

Problems with the Story

Like the baptism before it, the story of Jesus' temptation has many problems that make it implausible. First, Jesus was alone in the wilderness, and his reported encounter and conversations with the devil were private. Accordingly, nobody could have recorded and reported them, especially verbatim quotations. Given the fact that Jesus left no diaries or memoirs; that the first gospel, Mark, provided no detail; that Matthew and Luke's gospel were written many decades after the reported death of Jesus; and that Jesus' disciples did not write any of the gospels;[4] one cannot help but wonder where these details came from.

Second, the whole world could not have been visible with the naked eye from any hill or mountain in Israel. Therefore, the devil could not

---

[4] For a discussion of the authorship of the gospels, see Chapter 12.

have shown Jesus from any such location all the kingdoms of the world and offer them to him in exchange for worship. This claim appears to reflect a common assumption by ancient peoples that the world comprises only all the areas their eyes could see.

Third, the promise by the devil to give Jesus the world in return for worship assumes that the world belongs to the devil who could dispense it and its riches at will. Although Jesus apparently accepted this assumption, it is false and directly contradicts the Bible, several passages of which assert the ownership by God of the earth and everything in it. For example, Genesis 1:1-2 states that, 'In the beginning God created the heavens and the earth' which was void, formless and dark and filled it with everything in it. Psalm 24: 1-2 affirms that, 'the earth is the LORD's, *and everything in it, the world, and all who live in it*; for he founded it upon the seas and established it upon the waters.'[5] Confirming this position, 1 Corinthians 10:25-26 reports Paul as telling the church to 'eat anything sold in the meat market without raising questions of conscience', since the earth and everything in it is the Lord's. Further, in Exodus 19:5, Yahweh told the people of Israel that if they fully obeyed him and kept his covenants, they would be his treasured possession, *although the whole earth is his.* Finally, Deuteronomy 8:18 enjoins the people of Israel to remember Yahweh who gives them the ability to produce wealth in confirmation of the covenant he made with their ancestors. Therefore, assuming such a being exists, the devil was not in a position to offer

---

[5] Emphasis added.

Jesus the world or its wealth – and Jesus should have known that, if he were divine.

Fourth, the temptation narrative rests on the belief that God wilfully subjects people to temptation in order to ascertain their faithfulness, and in so doing, may act in concert with the devil. In the Book of Job for example, God for no reason other than self-gratification, allegedly conspired with Satan to tempt Job, 'a blameless and upright man' who 'fears God and shuns evil'. On God's prompting and encouragement, Satan subjected Job to increasingly horrendous and wicked punishments – from the destruction of his wealth and livelihood, through the loss of all his children, to the loss of his health by means of a shameful illness – until the man was broken.[6] In another example, God reportedly tempted Abraham's faithfulness by demanding the sacrifice of his only son and the child of promise, a temptation Abraham passed by his readiness to commit filicide.[7] The belief that God tempts people is also apparent in the 'Lord's Prayer' that includes a supplication that God should not lead us into temptation but should deliver us from evil.[8]

Was God then acting in concert with the devil to tempt Jesus? The gospels report that the Spirit of God (which had just descended in the form of a dove) took Jesus into the desert so that he could be tempted. This was apparently to prove his suitability or readiness for the

---

[6] See Job 1-3.
[7] See Genesis 22:3-13.
[8] Matthew 6: 13; see also Luke 11: 4.

ministry ahead of him and appeared to show that God was in on the act. If Jesus were the son or incarnation of God, why would God need to tempt him? What would be the point of God indulging in meaningless self-verification? If the point of the temptation were to prove to the people that Jesus was faithful, able and ready to embark on his ministry of salvation, it would also be futile since Jesus was alone, and his supposed encounter and conversation with the devil were secret.

Nevertheless, God does not tempt people, whether to test their faithfulness or entice them to do evil. As the book of James 1:13, rightly (though in contradiction to other Bible passages, including the ones referred to above) says, 'When tempted, no one should say, "God is tempting me". For God cannot be tempted by evil, nor does he tempt anyone.' Moreover, being omniscient, God does not need to test people to know what they would do at any time and in any given situation. Were God to tempt people for faithfulness, and only becomes convinced one way or the other after they have passed or failed the test, it would imply that God was oblivious of the outcome of the test until its conclusion.

Fifth, if Jesus were divine, he would not need to fast in preparation for his ministry, since fasting is 'a penitential practice designed to strengthen the spiritual life by weakening the attractions of sensible pleasures.'[9] While fasting may be of benefit to ordinary and weak

---

[9] See 'Fast and Fasting', in FL Cross and EA Livingstone (eds.) *Oxford Dictionary of the Christian Church* (Oxford University Press 1974).

mortals in their quest for spiritual purity, strength and growth, it is doubtful that the Son of God, or the very incarnation of God, would have a similar need. Jesus himself seemed to support the view that fasting is not needful to a person who is close to God when he reportedly responded to accusations that his disciples – unlike the Pharisees and the disciples of John the Baptist – did not fast. According to Jesus, guests do not need to fast when the bridegroom is with them.[10] By this, Jesus appeared to mean that since his disciples were with him, they did not need to fast, although such a need might arise when he had left them. If Jesus' disciples did not need to fast because he was with them, while would Jesus need to fast when he was supposedly the embodiment and fullness of God Almighty?[11] In fact, apart from the temptation episode, Jesus did not appear to fast again throughout his life and ministry. This led to accusations against him of gluttony.[12] In this context, Jesus complained that the people were hard to please, and observed that, when John the Baptist lived an ascetic life, they said he had a demon; but when 'the Son of Man came, eating food and drinking wine, they called him a glutton and drunkard'.[13]

---

[10] See Luke 5: 33 – 35; Matthew 9: 14 – 16; and Mark 2: 18 –20.

[11] See Chapter 13.

[12] See Luke 7: 33 – 34. See also Matthew 11: 19.

[13] Luke 7: 33.

Sixth, the story of Jesus' temptation assume in line with popular and biblical[14] mythology, the existence of the devil as a supernatural power constantly challenging God and seeking to thwart divine plans. Thus, the devil, as an adversary of God, came to tempt Jesus in order to derail his mission of salvation. The reality, of course, is that there is no supernatural being known as the devil, Satan, or by any other name; and there is no other power contending with God for supremacy.[15] If the devil does not exist, it follows that he could not have tempted Jesus in the wilderness. The most that could have happened then would have been contentions in Jesus' own spirit whether to follow one path or another – the kind of contentions human beings face regularly.

Finally, the gospel of John indicates that the story of Jesus' fasting and temptation most likely did not take place at all. In that gospel, there is no account of the fasting and temptation. Instead, at the same time that Matthew and Luke claim Jesus was alone in the wilderness, fasting and being tempted, Jesus was busy doing other things. First, he attended a wedding feast in Cana where he turned water into wine.[16] A day after the wedding feast, Jesus went away with his mother, brother, and disciples to Capernaum where they stayed for a

---

[14]Job 1, 2; Revelation 12; 1 Chronicles 21: 1; Isaiah 14: 12; Zechariah 3: 1 – 2; Matthew 25: 41.
[15] See LE Modeme, *Fantasy of Salvation* (Ameze Resources Ltd. 2019).
[16] In Cana, Jesus reportedly turned water into wine.

few days.[17] From Capernaum, he travelled to Jerusalem for the Passover and while there, drove traders away from the temple.[18]

A Classic Religious Tale

The temptation of Jesus appears to be little more than a tale designed to signal the displacement of Judaism and the inauguration of Christianity. The forty days and forty nights' stay in the desert, and the accompanying fasting, replicate the forty years of wandering by the Israelites in the wilderness following their exodus from Egypt,[19] and the forty days Israel's leaders spied over the 'promised' land.[20] It also replicates the forty days and nights stay and fasting in the desert by Moses and Elijah. However, Jesus' refusal to succumb to the temptations contrasts with the apparent submission of the Israelites to their own temptations and rebellion against Yahweh.[21] In addition, the episode shows a contrast in the attitude of Adam and Eve who succumbed to temptation and ate the forbidden fruit even in the midst of plenty in the Garden of Eden[22], and the attitude of Jesus who steadfastly obeyed God in very difficult situations. According to the Catholic Encyclopaedia:

> *Like Adam, Christ (the second Adam) endured temptation only*
> *from without, inasmuch as His human nature was free from*

---

[17] See John 1:36 – 2:1-12.
[18] See John 2:13.
[19] See numbers 32:13.
[20] Numbers 13:25.
[21] See Exodus 32; Numbers 14. See also See John Barton and John Muddiman (eds.) *The Oxford Bible Commentary* (Oxford University Press 2007), 851. See also WRF Browning (ed.) *Oxford Dictionary of the Bible* (Oxford University Press 2009) 351-352.
[22] Genesis 3.

all concupiscence; but unlike Adam, He withstood the assaults of the Tempter on all points, thereby affording His mystical members a perfect model of resistance to their spiritual enemy, and a permanent source of victorious help.[23]

All these are theological themes designed to demonstrate that a new Saviour, who would displace Adam, Moses and Elijah, had arrived.[24] This 'changing of the guards' finds reiteration in the story of the transfiguration when the apparitions of Moses and Elijah reportedly appeared and flanked Jesus in witness and support of the re-affirmation of his status as God's beloved son to whom the people should listen.[25] The temptation story tries to make clear, not only that the authority and ministry of Jesus have displaced those of Moses and Elijah, but also that Jesus had the blessing and support of Yahweh and his Jewish alter egos in so doing. The handover was complete; the ministry could begin.

However, the overcoming of temptations by heroes is a common motif in religion. Thus in Islam, Prophet Mohammed reportedly faced many temptations aimed at derailing his ministry. These included the apparent cessation of Allah's revelations to him, an offer of wealth and kingship, ostracism, stoning and persecution, enticement by women, and battlefield injury. Not only did the prophet overcome these temptations, he prayed for his persecutors and those working against his ministry.[26] In Buddhism, Gautama Buddha overcame

---

[23] http://www.newadvent.org/cathen/14504b.htm.

[24] See, e.g., the *Roman Catholic Catechism,* number 539.

[25] Matthew 17: 1 – 5.

[26] For a discussion of these, see T Andrae, *Mohammed: The Man and His Faith* (Dover Publications Inc. 2000).

attempts by demons to tempt him with beautiful women.[27] Similarly, the Bible's Old Testament gives accounts of Jewish heroes overcoming tough and challenging temptations. Abraham's faith was tested by a demand that he should sacrifice his only son and the child of promise, Isaac – a test he apparently passed by his willingness to carry out the sacrifice.[28] Jephthah proved his mettle by fulfilling his promise to sacrifice his daughter,[29] while Moses[30] and Elijah[31] withstood fasting for forty days and forty nights. For Jews, the stories of these and other heroes remain testimonies of the everlasting validity of the religious traditions and edicts they believe their God gave to them.

---

[27] See https://www.britannica.com/topic/Mara-Buddhist-demon.
[28] Genesis 22:1-19.
[29] Judges 11:30-40.
[30] Exodus 24: 18; Exodus 34: 28.
[31] 1 Kings 19:8.

CHAPTER 6

DID JESUS HAVE TWELVE DISCIPLES?

And when He had called His twelve disciples to Him, He gave them power over unclean spirits, to cast them out, and to heal all kinds of sickness and all kinds of disease. – Matthew 10:1

The selection of twelve disciples to be witnesses of, and partakers in, his ministry was the first action Jesus reportedly took after he began preaching following his baptism and temptation. These disciples were the people supposedly closest to Jesus in the course of his life and observers of all the major events concerning him and his ministry. In addition to the twelve, Jesus also sent out seventy disciples on the first evangelical mission recorded in the gospel. When Jesus departed the scene, this select group of men would supposedly lead the movement to spread his message of salvation to the world. How did Jesus select these men? Were they historical figures, or were they mythical or allegorical characters?

The Gospel Story: A Study in Contradictions
The gospels differ widely in their accounts of how Jesus chose his twelve disciples. Concerning the first disciples whom Jesus called,

Luke's story is significantly and substantially different from the stories of Mark and Matthew, while the story of John is completely different from the rest. In fact, the stories are so different that they could hardly be referring to the same persons or events.

In Luke, the first set of disciples Jesus called were Simon and the two sons of Zebedee, and preceding this call was a miraculous catch of fish. In this account, Jesus was preaching to a large crowd by the Lake of Gennesaret when he spotted two empty boats by the edge of the lake. He got into one of the boats, which happened to belong to Simon, and asked him to move the boat a little further inwards so that he would speak to the crowd from there. After speaking to the crowd, Jesus asked Simon who, with his fishing partners – James and John, the sons of Zebedee – had not been able to catch any fish all day, to move to a deeper part of the lake and cast his net. Upon doing as instructed, Simon netted so many fish that his net bulged to a breaking point, and he had to call for the help of James and John, and other nearby fishermen, to help pull the net. The catch from that single attempt over-filled two boats so that they began to sink. Overwhelmed by what he had just witnessed, Simon fell to the feet of Jesus, confessing that he was a sinner, and not worthy to be before him. Jesus then told him that from thenceforth, he would be catching men instead of fish. At once, Simon, James and John left their boats and other belongings, as well as the monumental haul of fish, and followed Jesus.[1]

The accounts of the first disciples in the gospels of Mark[2] and Matthew[3] are identical but are almost entirely different from Luke's narrative. In both, Andrew was fishing with his brother Simon in the Sea of Galilee when Jesus saw them. Without much ado, Jesus said to them 'Come, follow me and I will make you fishers of men'. Immediately, they left everything and followed Jesus. Here, Andrew and his brother Simon followed Jesus at the same time; but James and John, the sons of Zebedee, were not fishing with them. There was no crowd listening to Jesus, and no miraculous catch of fish.[4]

The story in John's gospel about the first disciples is completely different from that of the synoptic accounts.[5] According to this gospel, Andrew was a disciple of John the Baptist; and he, with another disciple, was with John somewhere[6] when Jesus passed by. John the Baptist said to his disciples, 'look, the Lamb of God'. On hearing this, Andrew and the other disciple left John and followed Jesus. The first thing Andrew did, the story continues, was to find his brother Simon and tell him that he had found the Messiah. He then took Simon to

---

[1] Luke 5: 1-11.
[2] Mark 1: 16-20.
[3] Matthew 4: 18 -22.
[4] Matthew 4: 18-20.
[5] John 1: 40-42.
[6] Presumably, this place was not Galilee because in the next verse (verse 43), we are told that, 'the next day, Jesus decided to leave for Galilee' where he found his next disciple, Phillip.

Jesus. Jesus promptly changed Simon's name to Cephas.[7] The differences between John's account and the synoptic accounts include the following:

1.   In John, unlike in the synoptic accounts, there was no indication that Simon and Andrew were fishermen; and they were not engaged in fishing when they met Jesus.

2.   According to John, it was Andrew and Simon who found Jesus. In the synoptic accounts, it was Jesus who found them.

3.   John claims that Andrew was called before Simon; whereas Matthew and Mark say they were called together. There was no mention of Andrew in Luke.

4.   John says that Andrew was a disciple of John the Baptist and was with the latter when he met Jesus. In Luke and Matthew, Andrew was nobody's disciple and was fishing with his brother Simon when Jesus saw them.

5.   In John, Jesus changed Simon's name to Cephas (Peter); there was no such name change in the three synoptic accounts.

6.   According to John, Andrew readily identified, and Simon readily accepted, Jesus as the Messiah. There was no such identification in the synoptic accounts.

7.   In John's gospel, John the Baptist pointed Jesus out to Andrew and his other disciples as the Lamb of God; there

---

[7] Which, when translated, is Peter.

was no mention of John the Baptist in the synoptic accounts.

There are even more contradictions and confusion regarding the second and third sets of disciples, as the gospels again do not agree on whom they were, or the manner in which they were called. According to Mark and Matthew, the next disciples Jesus called were James and John, the sons of Zebedee (the disciples already called, according to Luke). After Jesus' encounter with Andrew and Simon, he had gone away and later saw James and John, the sons of Zebedee, who were fishing with their father (not with Simon as Luke claims). Following their call by Jesus, the brothers left their father and everything they were doing and followed Jesus.[8]

Contradicting Mark and Matthew, John says that the second disciples called were Phillip and Nathaniel. Jesus had seen Phillip in Galilee and asked that he followed him. Phillip obliged, then found Nathaniel and told him that, 'we have found the one Moses wrote about in the Law, and about whom the prophets also wrote – Jesus of Nazareth, the son of Joseph.' Nathaniel followed Phillip to Jesus who disclosed to him what had earlier transpired between himself and Phillip. Nathaniel then declared, 'Rabbi, you are the Son of God; you are the King of Israel.'[9] Which of these accounts should one believe? The Gospel of Matthew identifies Matthew as the third disciple in the

---

[8] Matthew 4: 21-22.
[9] John 1: 43-50.

chronology of calls, while Mark and Luke identify him as Levi.[10] There is no indication that these were the same person; and there was no call of Matthew in the gospel of John.

Mark and Luke relate that Jesus chose the twelve from a body of disciples he had already assembled. However, apart from the disciples whose calls were above discussed, the gospels did not disclose who comprised this body of disciples, let alone how Jesus selected or called them. In Matthew, Jesus merely called together his twelve disciples in order to send them out on a mission. The names of the twelve disciples are given by the gospels as Simon (re-named Peter), James and John (the sons of Zebedee), Andrew, Philip and Bartholomew (John's gospel has a different person called Nathaniel). Others are Matthew (Mark and Luke mention a Levi), Thomas, James, the son of Alphaeus, Thaddaeus (Luke and the Acts have a Judas, the son of James) Simon the Zealot and Judas Iscariot.[11] Clearly, there are discrepancies and uncertainties in these names. Was Bartholomew in the synoptic gospels the same person as Nathaniel in John? Was Thaddaeus in Mark the same person as Jude the son of James in Luke and the Acts of the Apostles? Although often used interchangeably, it is also unclear whether Matthew the tax collector in Matthew's gospel was the same person as Levi in Mark and Luke. The gospels did not say, and there is no way of knowing with certainty, if they were the same or different persons.

---

[10] Matthew 9:9; see also Mark 2:14; Luke 5:27-28.
[11] See Matthew 10:2-4; Mark 3:16-19; Luke 6:13-16; Act 1:13.

In addition to the twelve, Luke's gospel[12] reports that Jesus sent out seventy disciples (or seventy-two in some manuscripts) on the first evangelical mission. However, that gospel, which is the only place in the Bible to mention the seventy disciples, is silent on the identities of these people. Meanwhile, the details given of their mission correspond to the mission of the twelve disciples in other gospels.[13] It is unclear therefore, if the missions and disciples are the same or different.

Significance of Numbers Twelve and Seventy

Why did the gospels record Jesus as choosing twelve disciples when he could have chosen any number of people other than twelve? Why did he send out seventy disciples, and not any other number, to preach? The gospels' choice of twelve would appear to be neither random nor accidental. It is consistent with the special place the number twelve has in Israel's national and religious tradition, which in turn has deep mythical and astrological roots.[14] Israel had twelve tribes representing the twelve sons of Jacob, the supposed immediate founder of the nation.[15] Ishmael, the son of Abraham through Hagar, like Jacob, also had twelve sons.[16] Joshua asked twelve men from each tribe to collect stones for alter-building after the Israelites had crossed

[12] Luke 10.
[13] See Mark 6:6-13; Matthew 9:35; 10:1.
[14] For the possible astrological origins of the story of the twelve apostles, see S Acharya, *The Christ Conspiracy: The Greatest Story Ever Sold* (Adventures Unlimited Press 2012), 166 – 167.
[15] Genesis 25: 29-34.
[16] Genesis 17:20. Genesis 25:12-15 give the names of the sons in the order of their birth as follows: Nebaioth, Kedar, Adbeel, Mibsam, Mishma, Dumah, Massa, Hadad, Tema, Jetur, Naphish and Kedemah.

the River Jordan;[17] and Yahweh asked the Israelites to bake twelve loaves of bread with fine flour for Sabbath offering.[18] In addition, twelve judges governed Israel before the advent of kings;[19] and the Qumran Monastic community[20] divided itself into twelve tribes headed by twelve overseers.[21] In the New Testament, Jesus was twelve years old when he reportedly confounded the scribes in the synagogue with his wisdom in his first and only appearance between infancy and ministry.[22] The New Jerusalem, according to Revelation, would have twelve angels guarding the twelve gates that would bear the names of the twelve tribes of Israel.[23]

This motif of twelve borrows from astrology and the myths of more ancient religions. The Zodiac has twelve stars or signs: Aries, Taurus, Gemini, Cancer, Leo, Virgo, Libra, Scorpio, Sagittarius, Capricorn, Aquarius and Pisces. These signs are supposed to represent the four universal elements of air, fire, water and earth.[24] In ancient Egypt, these zodiacal stars were the 'Saviours of the treasure of light' that

---

[17] See Joshua 4:1-4.

[18] Leviticus 25:5-6.

[19] The twelve judges of Israel were Othniel, Ehud, Shamgar, Deborah/Barak, Gideon, Tola, Jair, Jephtha, Ibzan, Elon, Abdon and Samson. See Judges 1, 3, 4, 5,6,10,12,13; Joshua 15:13-17; Joshua 19:15; I Chronicles 4:13; I Samuel 12:11; Hebrew 11:32.

[20] This First Century Jewish religious sect claimed to be the true Israel.

[21] See WRF Browning (ed.) *Oxford Dictionary of the Bible* (Oxford University Press 2009) 163-164. The sect, probably a part of the Essenes, lived on the banks of the Dead Sea. The Dead Scrolls found in 1947 in caves in that area, are generally attributed to them.

[22] Luke 2: 41-52.

[23] Revelation 21:12.

[24] See L Marshal (Rev.) ed., *The Mythical Life of Jesus* (Trafford Publishers 2011) 87-90.

accompanied the god Horus or Ra to the world.[25] Similarly, ancient Greeks had twelve major gods and goddesses in their pantheon. They knew these gods – Aphrodite, Apollo, Ares, Artemis, Athena, Demeter, Dionysus, Hades, Hera, Hermes, Poseidon, and Zeus[26] – as the Twelve Olympians because, apparently, they lived and held their councils on Mount Olympus. Even in Shia Islam, a much younger religion than Christianity, there are twelve Imams on whom leadership of the faithful fell after the death of Muhammad.[27]

The fact that the twelve disciples were meant to correspond with the twelve tribes of Israel is clear from the claim that the disciples would now be the judges of Israel.[28] To this effect, the New Testament asserts that the followers of Jesus, rather than the people of Israel as such, are now God's chosen people and nation.[29] Matthew's gospel goes as far as saying that Jesus Christ had promised the disciples that whatever they bound or loosened on earth would receive the same effect in heaven; and that heaven would honour whatever two or three of them agreed upon on earth in his name.[30] However, the equivalent

---

[25] See G Massey, *Ancient Egypt, The Light of the World: A Work of Restitution and Reclamation in Twelve Books*, vol. 1 (Routledge 2013) 782.

[26] See https://greekgodsandgoddesses.net/olympians/.

[27] See M Pearce, *Twelve Infallible Men: The Imams and the Making of Shi'ism* (Harvard University Press 2016).

[28] Matthew 19:28. See also See the entry, 'The Twelve' in BM Metzger and MD Coogan (eds.) *Oxford Companion to the Bible* (Oxford University Press 1993) 783. See further, the notes on Mathew 10:1-4 in *The New Oxford Annotated Bible, NRSV with the Apocrypha* (4th ed) (Oxford University Press 2010) 1760. , 1760; J Barton and J Muddiman (eds.), *The Oxford Bible Commentary* (Oxford University Press 2007) 858; WRF Browning (ed.) supra n 21, 164.

[29] See 1 Peter 2:9-10, Galatians 6:16; James 1:1.

[30] Matthew 18:18-19.

passages in the gospels of Mark and Luke do not contain these claims,[31] an unlikely omission if the claim was factual.

The use of number seventy also appears to have Jewish traditional connotations. In Genesis, seventy nations apparently emerged from the offspring of Noah following the flood and disruption of the construction of the city of Babel.[32] Exodus claims that the total number of Israelites who originally settled in Egypt was seventy.[33] Furthermore, Moses selected seventy elders of Israel for Yahweh's empowerment in order to help him lead the Israelites through migration from Egypt.[34] He also took seventy elders, along with Aaron and his sons, to Mount Sinai where they allegedly met and drank with Yahweh.[35] In addition, Israelites were in exile in Babylon for seventy years.[36] The story of the disciples therefore appears to continue the attempt to displace the Jewish order and replace it with a Christian one, especially given that the disciples did not seem to have played any significant part in the spread of the gospel of Christ – the role for which they were supposedly chosen and prepared. Instead, Paul, who was never a disciple or follower of Jesus, undertook that responsibility.[37] If the tale of the disciples has done little credit to the story of Jesus, would that of his miracles prove more useful?

---

[31] Mark 8:27-29; Luke 9: 18-20.
[32] Genesis 10, 11. See also http://www.ldolphin.org/ntable.html; http://www.soundchristian.com/man/.
[33] Exodus 1:5.
[34] Numbers 11:16-30.
[35] Numbers 24:9-11.
[36] Jeremiah 25:11-12.
[37] See LE Modeme, *Fantasy of Salvation* (Ameze Resources Ltd. 2019).

CHAPTER 7

DID JESUS PERFORM MIRACLES?

Then a great multitude followed Him, because they saw His signs, which He performed on those who were diseased. – John 6:2

Amiracle is something that 'causes wonder and astonishment, being extraordinary in itself and amazing or inexplicable by normal standards'.[1] Miracles are, therefore, often regarded as manifestations of divine power and an endorsement of the mission or message of the person through whom they are performed. Accordingly, the Bible attributes many[2] miracles to Jesus and portrays some of them as signs that he is the Saviour of humanity. Did Jesus perform the miracles attributed to him? If he did, does this prove that he is the Saviour of humanity?

The Miracle Stories

The miracles of Jesus, as recorded in the Bible, are many and of different categories. A good number of those miracles demonstrate his power over nature, while others demonstrate power over illnesses, evil

---

[1] *Encyclopaedia Britannica,* http://www.britannica.com/topic/miracle#toc34085.
[2] At least 35 specific ones and numerous unspecific others are reported.

spirits and death. His first miracle was that of turning water into wine at a wedding in Cana, Galilee after the host had ran out of wine. The wine Jesus converted from jars of water apparently tasted better than the one originally served at the wedding. Jesus performed a couple of miracles involving unusual catch of fish, namely the huge haul by Peter before his call, and the huge 153 fish he netted after the resurrection.[3] He fed 5000 men (and presumably some women and children as well) with five loaves and two fish,[4] and in similar circumstances also fed 4000 men with seven loaves and a few fish.[5] He miraculously made Peter to catch a fish with a 4-drachma coin in its mouth with which to pay taxes,[6] and cursed a fig tree to wither because it had failed to bear fruits out of season.[7] Jesus also reportedly rebuked a storm to quietude,[8] walked on water,[9] and fasted for forty days and nights.[10]

Another major category of Jesus' miracles was healing. His first healing miracle, by pronouncement, was that of a 'royal official's' son at Capernaum who was sick with fever.[11] Jesus also healed Peter's mother-in-law of fever by a rebuke and order,[12] and several people of

---

[3] See Luke 5:3-10; John 21:4-11, and Chapter 5.
[4] See Mark 6:30-44; Luke 9:10-15; Matthew 14:13-21.
[5] Matthew 15:29-39; Mark 8:1-10.
[6] Matthew 17:24-27.
[7] Mark 11:12-14, 20-21
[8] Matthew 8:23-27; Mark 4:35-41; Luke 8:22-25.
[9] Matthew 14:22-33; Mark 6:45-52; John 6:16-21.
[10] See Matthew 4:1-11; Luke 4:1-13.
[11] John 4:46-54.
[12] Matthew 14-15; Mark 1:29-31; Luke 4:38-39.

different illnesses by laying hands on them.[13] Furthermore, he healed a leprous man by laying hands on him and declaring that he should be clean. Although Jesus warned him not tell anyone about his healing, the man broadcast the miracle to everyone; thus, more people came for healing.[14] In addition, Jesus healed a paralysed man lowered into his presence through the roof,[15] a faithful centurion's son,[16] a man with a withered hand,[17] and a woman with a long-standing internal haemorrhage.[18] He also healed a cripple, whose predicament he attributed to sin,[19] as well as numerous people with various conditions at Gennesaret.[20] He healed a deaf man with speech impediment by inserting a finger in his ear and spitting on and touching his tongue;[21] and several blind people, including Bartimaeus.[22] Jesus' other healings include those of the woman who could not stand straight,[23] a man with dropsy,[24] ten lepers[25] and the restoration of the ear of the high priest's servant which had been severed by one of his disciples

---

[13] Matthew 8:16; Mark 1:32-34; Luke 4:40-41.
[14] Matthew 8:1-4; Mark 1:40-45; Luke 5:12-15.
[15] Matthew 9:1-8; Mark 2:1-12; Luke 5: 17-26.
[16] Matthew 12:5-14; Luke 7:1-10.
[17] Matthew 12:1-14; Mark 3:1-6; Luke 6:6-10.
[18] Matthew 9:20-22; Mark 5:25-34; Luke 8: 43-48.
[19] John 5:1-17.
[20] Matthew 14:34-36; Mark 6:53-56.
[21] Mark 7:31-37.
[22] See Matthew 9:27-31; Mark 8:22-26; John 9:1-41; Matthew 20:29-34; Mark 10:46-52; Luke 18:35-43.
[23] Luke 13:10-13.
[24] Luke 14:1-6.
[25] Luke 17:11-19.

during his arrest.[26] There were also healings of several people with unspecified diseases.[27]

Exorcism and raising dead people were the other important categories of miracles credited to Jesus. The Bible records that on many occasions, Jesus cast out devils and demons from those possessed. One of them was the man possessed by a 'legion' of demons that Jesus caused to enter a herd of two thousand pigs.[28] There was also the dumb man possessed by demons that Jesus healed and had his speech restored.[29] Other miracles of exorcisms include those of a Canaanite woman's daughter,[30] a boy suffering from seizures and falls,[31] and a blind and dumb man.[32] On the miracle of raising the dead, Jesus reportedly restored to life, the son of a widow at Nain,[33] Jairus' 12-year old daughter,[34] and the decomposing Lazarus.[35] In addition to the above, assorted miracles attended Jesus' crucifixion, including total solar eclipse, rending of the temple curtains, a large earthquake, and the resurrection of many dead 'saints'.[36] Jesus' final miracles were his resurrection from the dead and ascension to heaven.[37]

---

[26] Luke 22:45-54.
[27] Matthew 15:29-39; Mark 8:1-10.

[28] Matthew 8:28-32; Mark 5:1-13; Luke 8:26-33.
[29] Matthew 9:32-33.
[30] Matthew 15-21-28; Mark 7:24-30.
[31] Matthew 17:14-20; Mark 9:17-29; Luke 9:37-43.
[32] Matthew 12:22-23; Luke 11:14.
[33] Luke 7:11-17.
[34] Matthew 9:18-19, 23-25; Mark 5:22-24, 35-43; Luke 8:41-42, 49-56.
[35] John 11:1-44.
[36] See Chapters 8.
[37] See Chapters 9 and 10.

Problems with the Stories

Although believers see in the miracles of Jesus proof that he is the Saviour, a closer look reveals many problems with the miracle narratives that cast doubts on their occurrence and significance.

First, the accounts of many of the miracles in the gospels are contradictory. For a start, the first miracle of turning water into wine reported in John could not have happened according to the gospels of Matthew and Luke. This is because at the time of the said miracle, Jesus was praying and fasting in the wilderness and undergoing temptations by the devil.[38] Conversely, the miracle of fasting for forty days and nights preceding the temptation could not have happened according to John since at the time of the supposed events, Jesus was eating and drinking at Cana, and turning water into wine.[39]

With respect to the miracle of walking on water, Matthew and Mark report that Jesus instructed his disciples to leave him behind and go with the boat. However, John indicates that the disciples unwittingly left Jesus behind and sailed away in the boat.[40] If Matthew and Mark were right, the question arises as to why Jesus would ask his disciples to leave with the boat when there was no other boat for him to use. Conversely, if John were right, it would beg the question how the disciples would forget their master and depart with the boat. Further, Matthew reports that when Peter saw Jesus walking on the water, he

---

[38] See Matthew 4:1-11; Luke 4:1-13; John 1:40-42; and Chapter 5.
[39] Ibid.
[40] See John 6:16-21.

also went into the water to meet him but began to sink when he became afraid. There was no such occurrence in Mark and John. If this event actually happened, is it likely that they would omit it?

Concerning the miraculous feeding of 5000 men, the synoptic accounts state that Jesus fed the multitude because they had long been with him without food. On the contrary, John claims that Jesus decided to perform the miracle as soon as he saw the crowd of people coming towards him.[41] With respect to Peter's huge harvest of fish at the time of his call as a disciple, it is already evident that the gospels of Mark, Matthew and John contradict Luke on this event. Not only did they not record the fishing miracle, they gave a different account of the call of Peter.[42] Another implausible miracle was the catch of 153 huge fish by Peter when Jesus appeared to him after the resurrection. This incident could not have happened if we accept the post-resurrection narrative of Luke and Acts of Apostles according to which the disciples, as instructed by Jesus, waited in Jerusalem to receive the promised Holy Spirit.[43] When the Holy Spirit eventually came on the day of Pentecost, Peter and his fellow disciples did not go back to fishing but immediately went into the city, preaching and proclaiming the gospel.[44] Therefore, Peter, along with other disciples – James, John, Nathaniel and 'two others' – could not have been fishing in the Sea of Galilee when they were in Jerusalem waiting for

---

[41] See John 6:5-13.
[42] See Chapter 6.
[43] See Luke 24:49; Acts 1:4, 8.
[44] See Chapter 9.

the outpouring of the Holy Spirit. In fact, at the time of the alleged miracle, Jesus – according to Mark and Luke – had already ascended to heaven.[45]

Second, and as clear from the accounts above, the miracles performed by Jesus in the synoptic gospels were largely different from those reported in the gospel of John. For example, while the synoptic gospels narrate many miracles of exorcism, John did not mention any of them. Given the number of these miracles and their importance to the ministry of Jesus, it is incredible that John would ignore all of them. Conversely, the spectacular miracle of the resurrection of Lazarus, who had been dead for days and narrated in John, did not feature in the synoptic gospels. Considering the apparent closeness of Lazarus' family to Jesus and the magnitude of the miracle, one would expect that both Lazarus and his sisters would be popular in the earliest Christian circles. It is therefore, curious that the synoptic gospels written well before John's gospel[46] would omit this miracle altogether while recounting the relatively less important raisings of Jairus' daughter and the son of the unknown widow of Nain, which are not recorded in John. Moreover, the post-resurrection miraculous haul of 153 large fish in John did not appear in any other gospel. If Peter and some of the other disciples were the beneficiaries of this miracle, it is improbable that the other gospels would have missed it. If the disciples of Jesus observed the same miraculous events, why

---

[45] See Mark 16:19; Luke 24:50-52 and Chapter 10.
[46] See Chapter 12.

were they so different in these gospels? Why did the synoptic gospels leave out miracles, which the later gospel of John reported?

Third, the identities of the beneficiaries of the miracles of Jesus are often neither stated nor known, the only exception being Lazarus, Jairus' daughter, blind Bartimeus, Peter's mother (healed of fever), and Peter's two large harvests of fish. In all other cases, the beneficiaries were merely identified as some man, woman, or people. This is curious, given that the disciples of Jesus, or persons close to them, supposedly penned the gospels. If Jesus had benefited so many people by his miracles, some of these people would expectedly have become his followers and therefore well acquainted with the disciples and earliest Christians. In addition, there are no contemporary, historical or objective reports of the miracles, as the only report of them are in the gospels written several decades after the events they purport to narrate by people who did not witness, hear or have first-hand knowledge of them, with the objective of glorifying Jesus. This absence of contemporary or historical accounts and the clamour of 'all the people' of Jerusalem that Jesus should be crucified[47] cast doubts on the veracity of the miracle stories.

Fourth, God was apparently the source of many of the ailments, which were the subject of Jesus' miracles. According to the Bible, the LORD forms the light and darkness and creates prosperity and disaster.[48] The Bible also states that the LORD gives sight and blindness as well as

---

[47] See Chapters 8 and 12.
[48] See Isaiah 45:5-7; Jeremiah 18:11.

speech, hearing, deafness and dumbness.[49] This begs the question why God would inflict people with diseases only for Jesus to come and heal them miraculously. Yet, while Jesus healed people apparently afflicted by the LORD, he attributed many of the afflictions to the devil or demons, even though these creatures do not exist.[50]

Fifth, what amounts to a miracle is often uncertain because many things ancient peoples regarded as miracles were the results of the application of natural knowledge not known to most people at the time.[51] As human beings have a divine connection that would potentially enable them to affect the world around them in great ways, those who are able to tap into this source are capable of accomplishing what others would consider miraculous or extraordinary. The great scientific and technological breakthroughs that we have in the modern world would seem like miracles to people who do not know the knowledge behind them. Yet, those who masterminded these inventions and breakthroughs are neither gods nor messiahs. Moreover, the ancients erroneously attributed many ailments and disabilities – physical and mental – to devilish or demonic attacks, even though they were due to biological, psychological or neurological factors.

Finally, there is a great contradiction as to why the miracles happened. On the one hand, the Bible, most notably the gospel of John, acclaims

---

[49] See Exodus 4:11, and Chapter 5.
[50] See LE Modeme, *Fantasy of Salvation* (Ameze Resources Ltd) 387-401.
[51] See EP Sanders, *The Historical Figure of Jesus* (London: Penguin Books 1995) 157-159.

the miracles as 'signs' of Jesus' divinity and messiahship, with the faith of the beneficiary playing little part in the outcome. Referring to Jesus' miracle of turning water into wine for example, John describes it as 'the first of the signs through which he revealed his glory; and his disciples believed in him'.[52] Similarly, in John, before Jesus healed the centurion's son, in his 'second sign', he pointed out that the people would not believe unless they see signs and wonders'.[53] John goes on to assert that many people followed Jesus because of the signs he performed.[54] With respect to the miracle of feeding 5000 men, John states that it was a sign that made observers to declare that Jesus was surely the expected prophet. The restoration of the sight of a blind man and the resurrection of Lazarus were also signs for the glorification of Jesus and the work of God.[55] Acts of the Apostles also describe the miracles as signs validating the ministry of Jesus.[56]

On the other hand, the synoptic gospels report Jesus as saying on several occasions that it was the faith of the beneficiaries that made the miracles possible.[57] It was apparently for this reason that he could not perform any miracles in Nazareth since his own townspeople did not have the requisite faith.[58] Underlining the position that the miracles were not signs of anything, Jesus insisted that he would not

---

[52] John 2:11.
[53] See John 4:48, 54.
[54] See John 6:2.
[55] See John 9:3-5; 11:4.
[56] See Acts 2:22.
[57] See e.g., Mark 5:34; Luke 7:50; 8:48; 17:19.
[58] See Mark 6:5-6; Matthew 13:57-58.

give the people any signs from heaven,[59] except 'the sign of Jonah'[60] in apparent reference to his death and resurrection. In furtherance of this, Jesus placed a gagging order on recipients of his miracles so that the public would not wise up to his status or mission. However, even if one were to take the miracles of Jesus as factual or signs from heaven, they would not be peculiar or prove messiahship since other people have apparently performed similar miracles both within and outside the Bible.

Miracles in Judaism

In the Old Testament, prophets such as Moses, Joshua, Elijah and Elisha reportedly performed all the types of miracles credited to Jesus. Moses wrought several plagues in Egypt, including turning all its rivers and waters into blood and his staff into a snake. He caused darkness to come upon the whole land of Egypt and all the firstborns in the country to die.[61] Moses also parted the Red Sea,[62] healed the waters of Marah,[63] struck water from a rock,[64] and healed snakebites with a bronze snake sculpture.[65] Perhaps, most importantly, Moses regularly and physically communed with Yahweh who apparently wrote and handed him the Law on Mount Sinai – a privilege given to no other person in the Bible.[66]

---

[59] See Mark 8:12-13.
[60] See Matthew 16:4.
[61] See generally, Exodus 7 – 11.
[62] See Exodus 14:21-22, 26-28.
[63] See Exodus 15:25.
[64] See Exodus 17:1-17.
[65] See Numbers 21:8-9.
[66] See e.g., Exodus 19:16-18; 24:1-18; 24:12, 18; 39:29-35.

Like Moses, Joshua caused the River Jordan to part so that the Israelites would pass on dry ground.[67] He caused the city of Jericho to fall into the hands of Israel by mere marches and the blowing of trumpets,[68] and made the sun and the moon to stand still.[69] Perhaps, Joshua's greatest miracle was leading an unarmed people into other peoples' land after conquering their armies and overcoming their fortifications.

Another notable Old Testament miracle worker was Prophet Elijah. According to the Bible, this prophet reportedly caused rain to cease in Israel for over three years and to fall again.[70] He called down fire from heaven on at least three occasions.[71] During famine, Elijah received nourishment respectively from ravens[72] and a widow whose handful of flour and a small jar of oil lasted for years.[73] Elijah also parted the River Jordan[74] and raised the dead son of his host.[75] In addition to these miracles, Elijah reportedly made a number of accurate prophecies concerning Ahab's descendants[76] and King Ahaziah, and ascended to heaven alive in a whirlwind.[77] Elisha, the prophet who succeeded Elijah, reportedly performed even more miracles than his

---

[67] Joshua 3:14-17.
[68] Joshua 6:6-20.
[69] Joshua 10:12-14.
[70] 1 Kings 17:1; 18:41-46.
[71] 1 Kings 18:38; 2 kings 1:10, 12.
[72] 1 Kings 17:2-6.
[73] 1 Kings 17:12-15.
[74] 2 Kings: 2:8.
[75] 1 Kings 17:22.
[76] 1 Kings 21:22; 2 Kings 1:4.
[77] 2 Kings 2:10; 2 Kings 2:11.

master did, having received a double portion of his powers.[78] He replicated Joshua and Elijah's miracles of parting River Jordan,[79] healed River Jericho[80] and filled a valley with water.[81] He caused his barren host to get pregnant and have a son and later raised that son after he died.[82] He multiplied one vessel of oil into numerous vessels of oil[83] and fed 100 men with 20 loaves of bread with some leftover.[84] Elisha caused an iron axe head to float in the river,[85] proclaimed the beginning and end of a drought and famine,[86] and caused the Aramean army to become blind and later restored their sight.[87] Elisha also healed a leper,[88] caused bears to devour a group of forty-two jeering boys,[89] and inflicted a man with leprosy.[90] Elisha was apparently so powerful that a corpse came back to life upon coming into contact with his bones.[91]

Apart from the above examples, the performance of miracles appeared to be common among ancient Israelites, with many people reportedly

---

[78] 2 Kings 2:10.
[79] 2 Kings 2:13-14.
[80] 2 Kings 2:19-22.
[81] 2 Kings 3:16-20.
[82] 2 Kings 4:15-17; 2 Kings 4:32-36.
[83] 2 Kings 4:1-7.
[84] 2 Kings 4:42-44.
[85] 2 Kings 6:5-7.
[86] 2 Kings 8:1; 2 Kings 7.
[87] 2 Kings 6:18, 20.
[88] 2 Kings 5:13-15.
[89] 2 Kings 2:23-24.
[90] 2 Kings 5:26-27.
[91] 2 Kings 13:21.

possessing the ability. Narrating the exploits of famous miracle workers, before and after Jesus,[92] E.P. Sanders observes that:

> *Jews were especially known as miracle workers. Josephus claimed that they inherited the wisdom from Solomon and so knew how to perform healings, especially exorcisms. Illness and irrational behaviour were often attributed to demon possession, and those who could exorcise demons were much in demand. In a population in which the mentally unstable lived with relatives, not in asylums, many people would follow exorcists. And, such is the power of belief, or of mind over body, that cures were actually performed.*

Miracles in Christianity and other Religions

The Bible's New Testament records the disciples of Jesus, and Apostle Paul, as performing miracles, including healing the sick, casting out devils and demons and raising the dead.[93] So powerful were they in this respect, that the shadow of Peter and items that had touched Paul's body manifested extraordinary healing powers.[94] Moreover, church tradition and practice ascribe numerous miracles to saints,[95] with the certification by the papacy of miracles occurring in their name or through their relics being a pre-condition for beatification and canonisation.[96] Indeed, in our time, numerous

---

[92] EP Sanders, supra n 51, 138 -142.
[93] See Luke 10:17; Acts 3:6-8; 5:12-15; 9:33-34; 40-41;14:8-10; 16:16-18; 20:9-12; 28: 3-6, 8.
[94] See Acts 5:15-16; 19:11-12.
[95] See the *Catholic Encyclopaedia,* http://www.newadvent.org/cathen/09128a.htm.
[96] See the *Catholic Encyclopaedia,* http://www.newadvent.org/cathen/02364b.htm.

Christian preachers have laid and still lay claim to the performance of miracles such as healings, exorcisms and raising the dead.

In Islam, although Prophet Muhammad apparently refused to prove himself by miracles and wonders, Islamic tradition credits him with many miracles. Among others, he caused the moon to divide into two, multiplied water and date palms, and caused rain to fall and cease. Apparently, even trees and animals recognised Muhammad as the prophet of God. In addition, while still alive, the prophet ascended to heaven where he met Jesus, Moses and other prophets before him.[97] However, Moslems regard the writing of the Quran as the greatest miracle ever in that it was dictated by God, written down verbatim by the prophet over a period of about 23 years, and has remained uncorrupted for over 1400 years.

According to Hindu tradition, Lord Krishna, the eighth incarnation or avatar of Vishnu, performed many incredible miracles. He held up aloft Mount Govardhan (which was up to 26 miles in diameter) with one finger for seven continuous days in order to save the people of Braj from inevitable destruction by heavy rainfall. He manifested in the same form in numerous places at the same time, and was therefore able to stay with his 16,108 wives in different places at the same time. Lord Krishna also made the sun to rise and fall as he wished, healed

---

[97] See Sahih-al-Bukhari (a collection of Islamic oral traditions), Vol. 6, Bk. 60, No. 388; Vol. 1 Bk. 7, No. 340; Vol. 4, Bk. 56, No., 777, 779, 780; Vol. 8, Bk. 73, No. 115; Vol. 4, Bk. 54, No. 462; Vol. 5, Bk. 58, No. 227, 228; Vol. 3, Bk. 39, No. 517; Vol. 4, Bk. 56, No. 783. http://www.sahih-bukhari.com/Pages/Bukhari_1_07.php.

diseases, raised the dead, and overpowered demons.[98] These are only examples of the tales of miracles, which are prevalent in the legends of many religions – major, minor or traditional[99] – and found only in their respective scriptures or traditions for the purpose of validating their heroes and consolidating belief.[100] They are objects of faith insusceptible to objective verification.[101]

Miracles outside Religion

Outside the sphere of organised religion, tales of miracles also abound as magicians and medicine men perform them. The Bible for example recounts the tale of Simon Magus, a magician who 'amazed all the people of Samaria' with his sorcery, so much that they declared that he 'is rightly called the Great Power of God'.[102] It also recounts how the magicians of Pharaoh were able to replicate by their 'secret arts' many of the miracles Moses performed by the power of Yahweh.[103] Furthermore, history recounts the miraculous exploits of Jesus ben Pandira, an end-time Palestinian preacher, who lived between 106-79 BC and was crucified on the eve of Passover.[104] To this day, magicians and illusionists perform seemingly wondrous and miraculous feats,

---

[98] See http://www.lovekrishna.com/miracles-of-Lord-krishna.php.

[99] GF Chesnut, *Images of Christ: An Introduction to Christology* (Seabury Press 1984) 89.

[100] For a comparative examination and analysis of miracles in major religions, see G Twelvetree, *The Cambridge Companion to Miracles* (Cambridge University Press 2011).

[101] See generally, *Encyclopaedia Britannica*, http://www.britannica.com/topic/miracle#toc34085.

[102] See Acts 8:9-11.

[103] See Genesis 7:10-12, 22; 8:7

[104] See F Josephus, *Antiquities of the Jews* (Acheron Press 2012) 6:3.

including walking on water and fire, climbing tall building walls with bare hands and feet, going without food and drink for several weeks, etc. to the amazement of their audience and observers.

In traditional societies and folklore, medicine men or native doctors reputedly perform miraculous feats, such as turning into animals, flying in the air, being in different places at the same time, and causing rain to fall or cease. Yogis, monks and ascetics have been known to achieve extraordinary feats including walking bare foot on fire, lying on beds of nails, going without food for very long periods, and surviving after being buried alive for many weeks. In fact, unbelievers could reasonably describe many of the miracles credited to Jesus as magic in that they involved no apparent prayers. Perhaps, it was because of this that the Pharisees accused Jesus of performing them through the power of Beelzebub, the so-called prince of devils.[105]

Indeed, even devils and demons receive credit for amazing miracles. So strong was the belief in the power of the devil to perform miracles that, as already noted, the Jews accused Jesus of performing his miracles through the devil's power. The Bible describes the devil as the ruler or god of the world[106] who was able to offer Jesus all the kingdoms of the world in return for worship.[107] It also describes the devil as camouflaging as an angel of light,[108] while the Church credits him with advance knowledge of the mission of Jesus Christ and

---

[105] See Matthew 12:22-28.
[106] See John 14:30; 2 Corinthians 4:3-4.
[107] See Chapter 5
[108] See 2 Corinthians 11:14.

counterfeiting it in the doctrines, rituals and practices of more ancient religions, it considers pagan.[109] The book of Revelations warns that demonic spirits and false prophets using the power of the devil would perform amazing miracles, thereby deceiving many,[110] while some Christian sects believe that mainstream Christianity is a counterfeit created by the devil.[111] If the devil, demons, and numerous characters within and outside religion could perform miracles, any performance of such feats does not prove anyone a messiah. In any case, there is no evidence outside the contradictory and inconsistent gospel accounts that Jesus performed any miracles.

---

[109] See EG White, *The Spirit of Prophecy: The Great Controversy Between Christ and Satan*, Vol. IV, 1969 (Washington: Review and Herald Publishing Association 1969). See also https://www.tomorrowsworld.org/booklets/satans-counterfeit-christianity/content.

[110] See Revelations13:11-14; 16:14; 19:20.

[111] See e.g., EG White, supra n 109;

http://www.tomorrowsworld.org/booklets/satans-counterfeit-christianity/content.

CHAPTER 8

WAS JESUS CRUCIFIED?

Jews demand signs and Greeks look for wisdom, but we preach Christ crucified: a stumbling block to Jews and foolishness to Gentiles. - 1 Corinthians 1:22-23

O f all major religions practised today, only Christianity claims that its putative founder was crucified as a ransom for the sins of the world. This crucifixion, preceded by betrayal, arrest and trial, is critically important in the scheme of Jesus' saving mission in that it underpins his acclaimed resurrection and ascension – the glorious culmination of his incarnation on earth. If Jesus were to be the bringer of salvation to humanity as the gospels claim, the story of his passion must be unimpeachable. Is it?

The Gospel Story

The story of the betrayal, arrest and trial of Jesus could be summarised as follows:[1] Judas Iscariot, one of the disciples of Jesus, had requested a bribe of thirty pieces of silver in order to betray Jesus to the Jewish religious authorities. One night, having received the money, Judas led

---

[1] See Mark 14; 15: 1-15; Luke 22; 23:1-24; Matthew 26 and 27:1-26; John 18; 19:1-14.

a band of temple guards, a cohort[2] of Roman soldiers and a multitude of people at night to the Garden of Gethsemane at the foot of Mount Olives where Jesus was with his disciples. On seeing the large armed crowd coming toward him, Jesus wondered aloud why they felt it necessary to come for him so heavily armed given that he was not leading a rebellion, was with the people and religious authorities regularly in the temple courts, and taught in public places.[3] Then, Judas identified Jesus by kissing him as pre-arranged. These events, which Jesus had predicted, took place shortly after he had observed the Feast of Passover and eaten the Last Supper with his disciples and inaugurated the Eucharist.

The arresting party took Jesus to the High Priest and elders (the Sanhedrin) and laid against him the charge of blasphemy. After the Sanhedrin trial, in which Jesus was beaten and condemned for admitting that he was the Son of God, the accusers took him to Pontius Pilate, the prefect of Judaea. Although initially, the charges were unclear, his accusers eventually settled for subversion, opposition of payment of taxes to Caesar, and claims that he was the king of the Jews – charges tantamount to treasonable felony against the Roman Emperor and punishable by crucifixion. It seems that from the outset, Pilate did not take the charges seriously and was convinced they lacked merit. In an apparent attempt to avoid making a decision, Pilate sent Jesus for trial before Herod, the ruler (tetrarch) of Galilee.

---

[2] See John 18:2-3.
[3] See Luke 22:52.

However, Herod felt unable to adjudicate the matter and, after making mockery of Jesus, returned him to Pilate.

Pilate pleaded with Jesus' accusers and the crowd to allow him set the accused free; however, the plea went unheeded. Instead, they vehemently insisted on the conviction and crucifixion of Jesus. Unable to convince the people, Pilate tried one more tactic: he asked them to choose a prisoner for release – Jesus of Nazareth or Barabbas, a convicted murderer and rebel leader. In one voice, the people demanded the release of Barabbas and the crucifixion of Jesus.[4] At this point, despite his conviction about the innocence of Jesus and the nightmare-induced pleas of his wife,[5] Pilate acceded to the people's desire. After scourging Jesus and denying responsibility for it by washing his hands, Pilate sentenced him to death by crucifixion. Then putting a mock royal robe and a crown of thorns on him, he handed Jesus over for execution.

From Pilate's quarters, the execution squad marched Jesus to Golgotha, the place of crucifixion, commandeering along the way, a certain Simon of Cyrene to carry the cross. At Golgotha, the executioners offered Jesus wine laced with myrrh – a concoction to help deaden his pain – but he refused to take it. Then, the soldiers removed, cut and shared his clothes and cast a lot for his inner garment. On the third hour, they crucified Jesus along with two other criminals. On top of his cross were inscribed words meaning 'Jesus of

---

[4] See Matthew 27:15-26; Mark 15:6-8.
[5] See Matthew 27:19.

Nazareth, King of the Jews'. These words depicted the offence of treason for which he was crucified. The casting of the lots and sharing of garments were apparently in fulfilment of the prophecy that, 'they divided my garments among them and cast lots for my clothing'.[6]

While on the cross, the soldiers, chief priests and passers-by mocked and insulted Jesus, goading him to save himself as he had saved others. On the ninth hour,[7] Jesus died. His death was rather swift, such that there was no need to break his legs in order to hasten it. To ascertain that Jesus was already dead, a soldier pierced the side of his body with a spear, leading to the gushing out of blood and water. Apparently, all these happened in order to fulfil the prophecies that, 'Not one of his bones will be broken,' and, 'They will look on the one they have pierced'.[8] The death of Jesus happened on 'the day of Preparation, and the next day was to be a special Sabbath'. The Jews had requested the legs to be broken so that the bodies would not stay on the cross during the Sabbath.[9] Between being nailed to the cross and death, Jesus reportedly uttered different words.

Shortly before Jesus' death, the synoptic gospels report some extraordinary occurrences: the veil in the temple (shielding the holy of holies) tore into two halves and a total solar eclipse plunged the

---

[6] See John19:24.
[7] This is equivalent to 3 pm.
[8] See John 19:36-37. The scriptures alluded to here were Exodus 12:46; Numbers. 9:12; Psalm 34:20; and Zechariah 12:10.
[9] See John 19:31.

land into complete darkness.[10] In addition, a powerful earthquake shook the land, split rocks and opened graves, with many dead saints rising from their graves, and later (after Jesus' resurrection) walking the streets and appearing to many people in Jerusalem.[11] After his death, a certain Joseph of Arimathea, having obtained permission to take and bury the body of Jesus, wrapped it in a linen cloth, placed it in a rock-hewn tomb and rolled a big stone over the entrance.

Problems with the Story

Notwithstanding its indispensable doctrinaire significance and sentimental value to Christianity, a close look reveals many problems that make the Passion narrative extremely dubious.

The Last Supper

The synoptic gospels relate that the arrest of Jesus took place on the eve of Passover shortly after he had eaten the Last Supper with his disciples and given them the Eucharist. However, the gospel of John tells a different story. According to it, Jesus inaugurated the Eucharist early in his ministry while he was teaching in the synagogue at Capernaum. On that occasion, Jesus told his Jewish listeners – disciples and non-disciples alike – that he was the bread of life; and that they should eat his flesh and drink his blood. This bread, unlike the Manna eaten by their ancestors, would guarantee them eternal life. This teaching proved so objectionable that many disciples of Jesus

---

[10] See Luke 23:44-49.
[11] See Matthew 27:52-53.

other than the Twelve deserted him.[12] Although there was a meal 'just before the Passover festival' in John's gospel, it was not 'the Last' Supper, and there was no Eucharist in it. Instead, it was the occasion when Jesus washed his disciples' feet.[13]

If the Last Supper and Eucharist had happened as claimed, the disciples who witnessed it would not mix up the details or the time of its occurrence. Indeed, instead of seeing the Eucharist as a historical event, Apostle Paul indicated that he received knowledge of it spiritually from 'the Lord,'[14] and likened it to the bread and wine offered by Melchizedek; and the blood covenant instituted by him and Moses.[15] It seems then, that the Eucharist of Jesus Christ was an attempt to replicate the Jewish belief that the shedding of blood, including that of humans, is essential for atonement and forgiveness of sins. It appears to be a religiously motivated attempt to show that the 'new covenant' of Christ has displaced the old covenants of Moses and Abraham.

Betrayal by Judas Iscariot

The alleged betrayal of Jesus by Judas Iscariot makes no sense. As earlier noted, Judas allegedly agreed secretly to give Jesus away for a sum of money ostensibly to avoid a public outcry against his arrest. Yet, Judas went with a crowd of people to effect the betrayal and

---

[12] See John 6:35-70.
[13] See John 13.
[14] See 1 Corinthians 11:23-26. See also D Fitzgerald, *Nailed: Ten Myths the Show Jesus Never Existed at All* (Lulu.com 2010).
[15] See Genesis 14:18-20; Hebrews 9:11-22.

arrest. Although the arrest took place at night, the trial before Pilate happened publicly in daytime before a crowd that demanded in unison for the crucifixion of Jesus. Even as the soldiers led Jesus away for execution, the throng seemed happy with the turn of events. This narrative does not square with the gospels' claim that Jesus went about doing good deeds, healing people and casting out demons, and was beloved by the masses.[16] What had become of the vast multitudes of people who had been following him and had been receptive of his preaching? Where was the multitude of people that had attended his triumphant entry into Jerusalem shortly before his Passion? Where were the numerous people he fed, healed and delivered from devils and demons?[17]

In addition to the above, the religious leaders must have known Jesus who preached in open places, synagogues and the temple from which he had chased away traders and moneychangers. He had also on numerous occasions reportedly engaged in heated exchanges and disputations with the religious elite from whose ranks the Chief Priest and members of the Sanhedrin were drawn. These leaders would not therefore need anyone to identify Jesus, or seek him out in a hidden place. If their wish were to avoid publicity in their arrest and trial of Jesus, they would not have proceeded to do these at the time of Passover, arguably the biggest and most important festival in Israel.

---

[16] See Matthew 9:35; Acts 10:38.
[17] See Mark 11:1-11; Matthew 21: 1-17; Luke 19:29-40; John 12:12-19.

At this time, families and pilgrims converged on Jerusalem in large numbers, making public disorder much more likely.

Conversely, if the crowd of people at the trial were happy with the conviction and crucifixion of Jesus, and if the trial before Pilate took place in clear day light, there would have been no need for the extra caution taken by the religious leaders to apprehend him at night. Moreover, although the synoptic gospels state that Judas betrayed Jesus by a kiss,[18] John insists that Jesus identified himself to Judas and others, adding that the very presence and words of Jesus caused the arresting party to fall to the ground.[19] The alleged betrayal is also inconsistent with the claim all through the New Testament that Jesus *came willingly to give himself up* as ransom for the sins of others.[20]

Death of Judas Iscariot

The inconsistent and contradictory accounts of Judas' death given by the gospels cast further doubts on the entire crucifixion story. According to Matthew, when Judas saw that Jesus had been condemned to death, he became very remorseful and returned his bribe to the chief priests. When they would not take the money, Judas dropped it on the floor and hung himself. The chief priests, deciding that it was not proper to keep the 'blood money' in the temple treasury, used it to buy the Potter's Field for the burial of foreigners. This, according to Matthew, was in fulfilment of the prophecy by Jeremiah

---

[18] See Matthew 26:48-49; Mark 14:44-45; Luke 22:47-48.
[19] See John 18:3-6.
[20] See Ephesians 5:2, 25; and Galatians 2:20.

that, 'they took the thirty pieces of silver, the price set on him by the people of Israel, and they used them to buy the Potter's Field, as the Lord commanded me'.[21]

However, the claim that the death of Judas and the events associated with it was a fulfilment of the prophecy in Jeremiah is a fabrication. The so-called prophecy referred to the purchase by Jeremiah, for seventeen shekels of silver, a plot of land belonging to his cousin who had mortgaged it for a loan. By buying the land, Jeremiah, who was the closest relative, enabled the repayment of the debt while at the same time keeping ownership of the land in their family, as tradition required.[22] This story in Jeremiah has no connection to the story of Judas or the betrayal of Jesus; it was not even a prophecy concerning a future event but a narrative of an event that had already taken place. A related 'prophecy' cited in some manuscripts of Matthew as the one fulfilled by the death of Judas, is the narrative in Zechariah concerning thirty pieces of silver and Potter's Field. In that narrative, Zechariah related the metaphoric relationship of a shepherd and his flock, the breaking of the relationship, the consequent abandonment of the flock by the shepherd, and the termination of the fellowship between Israel and Judah. In the midst of the narrative, Zechariah told his listeners:

> *If you think it best, give me my pay; but if not, keep it. So they paid me thirty pieces of silver. And the LORD said to me, "Throw it to the potter"—the handsome price at which they priced me! So I took the thirty pieces of silver and threw them*

---

[21] Matthew 27:9-10.
[22] See Jeremiah 32:6-10.

into the house of the LORD to the potter. Then I broke my second staff called Union, breaking the brotherhood between Judah and Israel.[23]

This story clearly had nothing to do with Judas, and like the preceding one, related an event that had already passed. In any case, there was no suicide by anyone, no purchase of a Potter's Field, and no qualms about keeping the thirty pieces of silver in the 'house of the LORD'.

Meanwhile, Acts of the Apostles has a different account of the death of Judas, what became of his blood money, and the acquisition of a field. During the process of replacing Judas, Peter told his brethren that Judas himself bought a piece of land with the thirty pieces of silver he had collected. However, he fell headlong on that land, bust his gut and spilled his intestines. According to him, everyone in Jerusalem heard this tragedy, and because of it, called the piece of land *Akeldama*, meaning, Field of Blood. This event, Peter said, was to fulfil the prophecy in Psalms 69 and 109: 'May his place be deserted; let there be no one to dwell in it,' and, 'May another take his place of leadership'.[24] Both Psalms are, however, lamentations and prayers of the psalmist who felt so overwhelmed and surrounded by troubles and enemies that he called for the imposition of the wrath and vengeance of God on those enemies. Some of the desired acts of vengeance were the desolation of the enemies' habitations,[25] the

---

[23] Zechariah 11:12-14.
[24] See Acts 1:15-20.
[25] Psalm 69:25.

shortening of their lives, and the forfeiture of their leadership positions.[26] They were not prophecies, and did not concern Judas.

More intriguingly, Apostle Paul suggests that Judas Iscariot was not dead as claimed. Instead, he indicated that Judas was still among the disciples when Jesus appeared to them after his resurrection. In 1Corinthians 15:3-5, Paul states:

> *For what I received I passed on to you as of first importance: that Christ died for our sins according to the Scriptures, that he was buried, that he was raised on the third day according to the Scriptures, and that he appeared to Cephas, and then to the Twelve [...].*[27]

If we bear in mind that Matthias did not replace Judas until after the reported ascension of Jesus,[28] and that this epistle pre-dates the gospels, it becomes clear that Paul was speaking of the original twelve, which included the supposedly dead Judas.

Irregular Trials

The claims relating to the trials of Jesus by the High Priest, Herod and Pilate are unrealistic. The trial before the Sanhedrin would be in serious contravention of the Jewish law that forbade such trials at night, and during the Sabbath, festivals and eves of festivals.[29] Moreover, being a charge of blasphemy that carried the death penalty, the full Sanhedrin of seventy-one people needed to meet. Even though

---

[26] Psalm 109:8
[27] Emphasis added.
[28] See Acts 1:9, 26.
[29] See http://www.jewishencyclopedia.com/articles/4766-criminal-procedure.

the gospels claim that, 'all the chief priests, the elders and the teachers of the law came together',[30] it is unlikely that all the members of this supreme court of Jewish Law would agree so flagrantly to break the law. This is especially so, considering that these leaders apparently refused to enter the palace of Pontius Pilate when they took Jesus there because they did not wish to be unclean for the Passover.[31] It is also unlikely that these eminent religious jurists would physically manhandle Jesus after condemning him, as alleged in the narratives.[32] In addition, although the gospels claim that the Sanhedrin was unanimous in its condemnation of Jesus, they go on to claim that a prominent member of that Council, Joseph of Arimathea, was a follower of Jesus who requested for his body and buried it in his own tomb.[33]

It is also unlikely that a person could have been charged, tried, convicted and sentenced for a capital offence in one day and the sentence executed on the same day, as the gospels claimed was the case with Jesus. These outcomes are even more unlikely, given that there was no prior notice or scheduling. Not only would such a state of affairs have been inconsistent with the formality of trial under Roman law, it would also be inconsistent with the facts alleged in the gospel story. Considering that Pilate was convinced of Jesus'

---

[30] See Mark 14:53. See also Matthew 26:57.
[31] See John 18:28.
[32] See generally, *The Jewish Encyclopaedia*, http://www.jewishencyclopedia.com/articles/13178-sanhedrin; H Cohn, *The Trial and Death of Jesus* (Konecky & Konecky 2000).
[33] See Mark 15:43; Matthew 27:57-60; Luke 23:50-53.

innocence and was eager to set him free; that Pilate's wife, who had nightmares about the case, had intervened in favour of Jesus; and that Jesus was also taken to Herod before being brought back to Pilate; the timeline of the trials is highly unnatural and unrealistic. The fact that Barabbas, earlier convicted of treason and murder, was still awaiting execution at the time of Jesus's own trial suggests that the Romans did not carry out executions following such convictions in undue haste. Further buttressing the unrealistic timeline is the anxiety of the Jewish authorities to conclude the trial and crucifixion before the commencement of the Passover Sabbath the same evening. Why the haste? Why could they not wait even for a few days? Why would Pilate indulge that haste?

Pontius Pilate

The account of the trial before Pilate dubiously and arbitrarily portrays the prefect as a weak, indecisive and malleable ruler who was beholden to his Jewish subjects. Although Jesus' accusers made allegations of treason, they kept changing the charges, and produced no evidence to substantiate any of them. Pilate not only knew that Jesus was innocent and that the charges against him were fabrications, he also publicly declared him not guilty. Notwithstanding all these, he condemned Jesus to death apparently in order to please the people. This portrayal of Pilate contradicts his true character and antecedents as attested in history and the Bible.[34] According to the Catholic

---

[34] See WRF Browning (ed.) *Oxford Dictionary of the Bible* (Oxford University Press 2009) 290.

Encyclopaedia, Pilate was an 'inflexible, merciless, and obstinate' ruler who was hated by the Jews because 'he was not only very severe, but showed little consideration for their susceptibilities'.[35]

Luke's gospel corroborates the statement about Pilate's wickedness and unconcern for the Jews by reporting that he had mingled their blood in sacrifices.[36] Furthermore, the renowned Jewish historian and friend of the Roman Emperor, Josephus, indicates that Pilate was a headstrong, strict and authoritarian ruler not concerned with the feeling of his subjects.[37] These characterisations of Pilate show that he was not likely to behave in the manner indicated in the gospel story. In any case, a Roman Chief Judge, as Pilate was, was not likely to condemn an accused person to death after finding, and publicly declaring him, innocent. That would have undermined not only his integrity, but also that of the Roman government and its judicial system that forbade the execution of a non-convicted person.[38] Conversely, if he felt that Jesus was guilty of subversion or treason, Pilate would have had no compunctions about condemning him to death and crucifying him, given that the Roman authorities had

---

[35] http://www.newadvent.org/cathen/12083c.htm.

[36] See Luke 13:1.

[37] See *Encyclopaedia Britannica,*
http://www.britannica.com/EBchecked/topic/460341/Pontius-Pilate. See also F Josephus, *Antiquities of the Jews* (Acheron Press 2012) Book XVIII, Ch.3.

[38] According to Law IX of the Twelve Tables *(Lex XII Tabularum)* of Roman law, already in existence at the time of Pilate, 'Putting to death of any man, whosoever he might be unconvicted is forbidden'. See *Encyclopaedia Britannica,*
http://www.britannica.com/EBchecked/topic/610934/Law-of-the-Twelve-Tables. See also the *History Guide*, http://www.historyguide.org/ancient/12tables.html.

crucified many people claiming to be the messiah and king of the Jews.[39]

The depiction of Pilate therefore appears to be an attempt by the gospel writers to exonerate the Roman authorities of responsibility for the crucifixion of Jesus and lay the blame on the Jews, even though the charge and execution were clearly Roman in nature.[40] Indeed some Christian sects, especially the Eastern Orthodox Church, and the Ethiopian Orthodox Church, claim that Pilate later became a pious Christian and a saint.[41]

The Passover Lamb

It seems that the gospel writers were eager to associate the death of Jesus with the Passover in an attempt to replace that festival with the commemoration of the death of Jesus. Reinforcing this notion is the fact that the Eucharist, which Jesus reportedly instituted at his last Passover meal, followed the order of the breaking of the Passover bread and the drinking from 'the cup':

> And he took bread, gave thanks and broke it, and gave it to them, saying, 'This is my body given for you; do this in remembrance of me.' In the same way, after the supper he took

---

[39] See *Jewish Encyclopaedia*, http://www.jewishencyclopedia.com/articles/4782-crucifixion. Perhaps, the story of Jesus' trial and crucifixion was an imitation of these historical incidents.

[40] See e.g., WRF Browning (ed.) *Oxford Dictionary of the Bible* (Oxford University Press 2009) 73.

[41] See *The Catholic Encyclopaedia*, http://www.newadvent.org/cathen/12083c.htm. See also *Encyclopaedia Britannica*, http://www.britannica.com/EBchecked/topic/460341/Pontius-Pilate.

the cup, saying, 'This cup is the new covenant in my blood, which is poured out for you.[42]

Therefore, the New Testament describes Jesus as the Passover Lamb in lieu of the lamb the Jews usually sacrifice and consume during the Passover.[43] For this reason, Paul urged the Corinthians to 'purge out the old leaven', and replace it with the new Passover meal – Jesus.[44] The New Testament also describes Jesus as the Lamb of God that takes away the sins of the whole world. The idea therefore is that just as the firstborns of Israel were spared in Egypt by the blood of the lamb used to mark their door posts, from then onwards, the Jews (and the world) would be saved through the blood of Jesus that was about to be shed. This posturing however, ignores the fact that the Passover Feast was instituted 'as an eternal covenant' between the Israelites and their God, and could therefore not be substituted by any person.[45]

The Release of Barabbas

The claims that Pilate released Barabbas, a convicted rebel and murderer, in furtherance of a custom, and that he condemned Jesus so that the Jews would not report him to Emperor Caesar as an enemy, further undermines the credibility of the trial narrative. Whereas the synoptic gospels claim that the custom was Roman, the gospel of John describes it as Jewish.[46] However, the Romans had no such custom

---

[42] Luke 22:19-20.
[43] See Deuteronomy 16:1-8.
[44] I Corinthians 5:7-8.
[45] See Exodus 12:14; 24-28; Leviticus 23:4-8.
[46] See Matthew 27:15; Mark 15:6; John 18:39.

and the Jews seem to know nothing about it,[47] as it was 'attested only in the New Testament'.[48] The alleged custom appears to be a forgery or an allegory depicting the ritual observed during the Day of Atonement, when the people cast lots for two male goats, after which they would kill one as a sin offering and release the other into the wilderness as a scapegoat for their sins.[49]

In addition, the claim in John's gospel that Pilate finally gave in to the crowd's demand to condemn Jesus so they would not report him to Caesar[50] holds no water. Pilate would not crucify Jesus, a person he publicly acknowledged to be innocent of the charge of treason, in order to set free Barabbas, a rebel and murderer. Would Caesar not be more upset with Pilate for setting free Barabbas in place of Jesus who had declared that his government was not of this world, and in whom he had found no fault?

Crucifixion on a Cross

Although the gospels claim that Jesus was crucified by being nailed on a cross, biblical reports other than in the gospels state that he was hung on a tree. In Acts 5:29-30, Jesus' disciples told their Jewish compatriots that, 'the God of our fathers raised up Jesus whom you murdered by *hanging on a tree'*, an accusation Peter and Paul repeated in Acts 30:39 and 13:29 respectively. In addition, 1 Peter 2:24 states

---

[47] See also, the *Jewish Encyclopaedia,*
http://www.jewishencyclopedia.com/articles/4782-crucifixion.
[48] See the explanatory notes on John 18:39-40 in *The New Oxford Annotated Bible, NRSV with the Apocrypha* (4[th]ed) (Oxford University Press 2010) 1912.
[49] See Leviticus 16:5-10, 15-22; D Fitzgerald, supra n 14, ch. 7.
[50] See John 19:12.

that Jesus, 'himself bore our sins in His own body *on the tree*', so that by his stripes we are healed. Lastly, Apostle Paul states that 'Christ has redeemed us from the curse of the law, having become a curse for us (for it is written, "Cursed *is* everyone who *hangs on a tree*").'[51]

So, is crucifixion on a cross the same as being hung on a tree? Not really. While crucifixion involves impaling or tying a person on a stake or cross,[52] hanging on a tree involves suspending the body from the tree. The Greek word *stauroo* used in the gospels for crucifixion is different from the word *prospēgnym* used in the Acts and the other passages in the New Testament to denote hanging.[53] Even if Bible writers have used these two words interchangeably, crucifixion is still different from hanging on a tree. If the Roman authorities had indeed killed Jesus, those who witnessed the killing, especially his disciples, could not be confused as to the exact manner of the death; neither would early Christians forget it. It is important to note that although the cross (with or without the crucifix) has since become the main symbol of mainstream Christianity, its use in various configurations was common among more ancient religions and cultures which the church describes as pagan. According to the Catholic Encyclopaedia:

> *The sign of the cross, represented in its simplest form by a crossing of two lines at right angles, greatly antedates, in both the East and the West, the introduction of Christianity. It goes back to a very remote period of human civilization [...] the cross was originally not a mere means or object of ornament,*

---

[51] Galatians 3:13.
[52] See http://www.newadvent.org/cathen/04517a.htm.
[53] See https://discover-the-truth.com/2013/07/16/was-jesus-hanged-or-crucified/.

and from the earliest times had certainly another — i.e. symbolico-religious — significance.[54]

In fact, the common use by Christians of the symbol of the cross did not start until the 4th Century CE following the 'conversion' of the Roman Emperor, Constantine.[55] Because of its pre-Christian origins, the shame and ignominy of crucifixion, and their insistence that Jesus did not die on a cross, some Christian denominations refuse to use the cross as a symbol of the religion.[56]

Jesus' Attitude to His Passion

The gospels give contradictory descriptions of Jesus' behaviour during his travails. During the trials, the synoptic gospels insist that Jesus did not say a word in response to the charges brought against him and to questions put to him.[57] In contrast, the gospel of John depicts a loquacious Jesus who engaged both the High Priest and Pilate in several verbal exchanges and reported verbatim his responses to Pilate's questions.[58]

Jesus' reaction to his impending crucifixion and death on the cross also differs widely in the synoptic and John's gospels. While the synoptic gospels show a human Jesus in pain and anguish bemoaning

---

[54] http://www.newadvent.org/cathen/04517a.htm. See also
https://www.britannica.com/topic/cross-religious-symbol.
[55] https://www.britannica.com/topic/cross-religious-symbol.
[56] See e.g.,
https://www.cgg.org/index.cfm/fuseaction/Library.sr/CT/ARTB/k/471/Cross-Christian-Banner-Pagan-Relic.htm;
https://www.jw.org/en/publications/magazines/wp20080301/Why-Do-Jehovahs-Witnesses-Not-Use-the-Cross-in-Worship/.
[57] See Matthew 27:11-13; Mark 15:2-5; Luke 23:3-4.
[58] See John 18:20-23, 33-38; 19:10-11.

his fate, John's gospel paints a picture of a super-human and calm Jesus unperturbed by the situation, oblivious to pain, and fully in charge of his circumstances. According to the synoptic gospels, shortly before his arrest, Jesus, while overwhelmed by sorrow, prayed to God to remove from him if possible, the cup of suffering and death. Luke adds that in his anguish Jesus sweated drops of blood.[59] The synoptic gospels also state that a certain Simon of Cyrene had to help Jesus with his cross,[60] and while on the cross, Matthew and Mark relate that Jesus cried and lamented his fate before giving up the ghost.[61] This was a Jesus of passion.

Conversely, John narrates that before his arrest, Jesus was not in any sorrow or anguish whatsoever. Instead, he was confident that he had overcome the world and accomplished his divine mission. He merely asked God to glorify him just as he had glorified God and prayed for his disciples and followers.[62] Contrary to the synoptic gospels' claim, Jesus made it clear that it would not lie in his mouth to ask God to remove the cup of suffering and death from him since it was for that glorious purpose that he had come to the world.[63] He further asserted that after his lifting up from the earth, he would draw people unto himself.[64] In John, Jesus needed nobody's help but carried his cross

---

[59] See Matthew 26:36-39; Luke 22:39-45; Mark 14:32-35.
[60] Matthew 27:32; Mark 15:21; Luke 23:26.
[61] See Mark 15:34; Matthew 27:46.
[62] See John 16, 17.
[63] See John 12:27-28.
[64] See John 12:32

by himself.[65] While on the cross, John relates that Jesus made no lamentation but remained in control, telling his beloved disciple to look after his mother. He only stated that he was thirsty 'so that scriptures would be fulfilled'. At the hour of death, Jesus simply declared, 'it is finished',[66] apparently to indicate that the choice to die at thát time was entirely his.[67] Unlike Jesus of the synoptic gospels', the Jesus of John was not one of passion at all.

The Two Criminals

The case of the two criminals allegedly crucified with Jesus poses more problems. Luke narrates that one of them insulted Jesus, taunting him to save himself and them, while the other was repentant, lambasted his brother-in-crime, and pleaded with Jesus to remember him when he came into his kingdom. Then Jesus promised to take the repentant criminal with him to Paradise.[68] The gospels of Matthew and Mark, however, flatly contradict Luke on this. In their own report, none of the robbers was repentant; none asked Jesus to remember him in his kingdom, and Jesus did not promise to be with any of them in Paradise. On the contrary, they report that both robbers joined the people in insulting Jesus. As they put it, not only did the soldiers and

---

[65] See John 19:17.
[66] See John 19:25-30
[67] See John 10:17-18.
[68] Luke 23:39-43.

others around insult Jesus, '*those* crucified with him also heaped insults on him'.[69]

Earthquake, Solar Eclipse and Risen Corpses

There are also problems with the claim that upon the death of Jesus on the cross, some wonders happened, including earthquakes, a solar eclipse, and the rising of corpses from their graves. However, there were no reports of these extraordinary events anywhere in Jewish or historical records. A violent earthquake that exhumed corpses could not have gone unnoticed or unreported; and if the earthquake was able to exhume bodies, it could have felled or destroyed houses and trees. Similarly, a total solar eclipse – an infrequent and important astronomical event – could not have gone without recording especially when it apparently lasted for hours. Yet, there is no report of this great eclipse anywhere other than in the Bible's New Testament. This eclipse seemed to have been associated with the death of Jesus in the same way as a shining star was associated with his birth.

Perhaps even more perplexing and incredible is the claim of re-animated corpses breaking through from their graves. If bodies of dead people got out from their graves, walked about on the streets for days in the presence of many people, these would be unforgettable events in the annals of Israel, if not the world. Who were these dead

---

[69] See Mark 15:32; Matthew 27:44. Although the gospel of John reports that two other people were crucified with Jesus, it did not say anything other thing about them.

and risen saints? What became of them eventually? Did they return to the grave, or did they go on to live as normal human beings? Why was there no report of this astonishing event anywhere other than in the gospels?

The Passion and Prophecies

The assertion in John's gospel that Jesus' quicker-than-expected death was in fulfilment of prophecies has no scriptural basis, as the passages cited do not have anything to do with Jesus or his death. Exodus 12:46 and Numbers 9:12 concern the preparation of the Passover lamb, the bones of which, according to Jewish tradition, must not be broken. Psalm 34:20 concerns the Psalmist's praise to Yahweh on his treatment of a righteous person. Among other things, Yahweh would deliver him from all his troubles and would not allow his bones to be broken. On its part, Zechariah 12, verses 1-9, was an assurance by the prophet that Yahweh would protect Jerusalem from its enemies and a prophecy of mourning for 'me, the one they have pierced'. These verses did not relate to Jesus and there is no indication that verses 10-13 applied to him, or that the incident of mourning referred to was relevant to his time. John also claims that when the soldiers who crucified Jesus disposed of his garment by lot, it was in fulfilment of the prophecy in Psalm 22:18 that, 'they divided my clothes among them and cast lots for my garment'. However, this is a long Psalm of general lamentation and supplication unrelated to Jesus or his crucifixion. The linking of these Old Testament passages to the death of Jesus is consistent with the practice of the gospel writers of picking random and inapplicable passages in the Hebrew Scriptures and connecting them to Jesus as fulfilled prophecies.

Dead for Three Days and Three Nights

Finally, the synoptic gospels record that the death and burial of Jesus took place on the preparation day (i.e. the day before the Sabbath).[70] Since Sabbath begins at sunset on Friday evening and ends just after sunset on Saturday evening, the preparation day for the Sabbath would therefore stretch from Thursday night to before sunset on Friday, although traditionally Friday is regarded as the preparation day. Where the Passover falls on a Sabbath, the preparation day would still be as indicated above – Thursday night to before sunset on Friday – and the people would slaughter the Passover lamb before sunset on the Friday. The eve of Passover would then be from Thursday night to the onset of sunset on Friday. By this calculation, Jesus died before sunset on Friday, just before the commencement of the Sabbath/Feast of Unleavened Bread. Accordingly, the Galilean women who were meaning to apply spices on his corpse, having noted the location of his tomb, returned home to observe the Sabbath.[71] After the Sabbath, they returned to the tomb in an attempt to apply the spices to the body of Jesus.[72]

However, the claim that Jesus died on Friday afternoon before the Sabbath is inconsistent with the timeline of events given in both the

---

[70] Mark 15:42-43.
[71] Luke 23:54-56.
[72] See Mark 16:1; Luke 24:1.

synoptic and John's gospels. In the synoptic account,[73] the arrest of Jesus took place on the night of the first day of the Feast of Unleavened Bread (Friday evening) after he had already eaten the Passover meal with his disciples.[74] After the meal, Jesus went with his disciples (minus Judas) to the olive groves – or Garden of Gethsemane – where, on the same night, the arrest and trial before the Sanhedrin happened.[75] Early the following morning (being Saturday), Jesus was taken before Pilate, where he was tried, convicted and despatched for execution.[76] His crucifixion took place on the same day, at about the sixth hour; and at about the ninth hour, he died.[77] By this timeline of events, the death and burial of Jesus would have been on Saturday, however, this would mean that the burial took place before the trial and crucifixion.

According to John's gospel, just before the Passover feast, Jesus had gathered with his disciples for dinner. This would be late afternoon on Friday.[78] In the course of this Passover meal, Jesus washed the disciples' feet, predicted his imminent denial by Peter and his betrayal by Judas. After the meal, Jesus proceeded with his disciples to the Garden of Gethsemane. While there, Judas and the crowd of armed people came to arrest Jesus. After the arrest, and on the same night,

---

[73] See Matthew 26:17-25 and 27:1-56; Mark 14:14-54; 15:1-27; Luke 22:7-71; 23:1-56.
[74] See Mark 14:12-13, 16.
[75] See Mark 14:53-54.
[76] See Mark 15:1-27.
[77] See Mark 15:33-37.
[78] See John 13:1-38.

they brought Jesus before Annas the father-in-law of the High Priest and to the High Priest for a Jewish trial. Early the following morning (which would be Saturday), they took Jesus to Pilate; and wishing to avoid ceremonial uncleanness that would debar them from eating the Passover, they refrained from entering Pilate's palace.[79] By this account, Pilate tried Jesus on Saturday, convicted and released him for execution the same day. That means that Jesus died and was entombed on Saturday. However, John states that Pilate tried and condemned him, and had him executed on 'the day of preparation of Passover Week.'[80] Since the preparation for the Passover week could not have gone beyond sunset on Friday, this suggests that Jesus' crucifixion and burial took place on Friday afternoon (about the sixth hour). This contradicts the earlier timeline of events given by John.

Nevertheless, even if we accept that Jesus died and was buried on a Friday afternoon and that he resurrected early on the following Sunday morning, that timeline would contradict the messiah sign apparently given by Jesus to the Pharisees and scribes. The sign was that he would stay three days and three nights in the grave – a period amounting to 72 hours. This was the 'sign of Jonah' in that he would stay under the earth for the same duration (i.e., three days and three nights) that Jonah stayed inside the belly of a great fish.[81] Burial on Friday afternoon and resurrection on Sunday morning would amount to two nights even if one reckons a small fraction of Friday evening,

---

[79] See John 18:28.
[80] See John 19:14-15; 31.
[81] See Matthew 12:39-40, Jonah 1:17.

Saturday, and a tiny fraction of Sunday morning as three days.[82] Clearly, therefore, the story of the passion of Jesus looks more like a fantastic religious drama than a narrative of real events. What about the story of his resurrection?

---

[82] See D Pack, 'Christ's Resurrection was not on Sunday', *The Restored Church of God*, http://rcg.org/books/crwnos.html.

CHAPTER 9

DID JESUS RESURRECT FROM THE DEAD?

And if Christ has not been raised, our preaching is useless and so is your faith. More than that, we are then found to be false witnesses about God, for we have testified about God that he raised Christ from the dead [...] – 1 Cor. 15:14-15

The resurrection of Jesus underpins the Christian faith and reassures believers that their redeemer lives on. If, as shown in the previous chapter, the crucifixion of Jesus might not have happened as claimed in the gospels, it would follow that the resurrection could not have happened either. However, due to its critical importance to Christianity and its scheme of salvation, the resurrection story deserves an independent examination. If, somehow, the resurrection did happen, it could go some way in keeping alive the hope that Jesus might after all be the Saviour, although questions would remain about its true significance given that such a story is not peculiar to him. If, however, the resurrection did not happen as claimed, the story of Jesus as the Saviour of humanity would continue irretrievably to unravel.

The Gospel Story

The gospels report that early in the morning of the first day of the week after Jesus' entombment, some female followers of his went to the tomb, either to look at his tomb, or to apply spices on his body. On getting there, they discovered that the stone previously covering the tomb did not cover it anymore, and that the body was no longer there. Apparently, Jesus had arisen. The gospels record that the risen Jesus appeared to the women who came to the tomb and to his disciples who touched him and ate with him many times. Subsequently, he spent time, varying from one day to forty days – depending on which account one reads – with the disciples.[1] Then, Jesus commissioned the disciples to preach the gospel globally as most dramatically stated in Mark's gospel:

> *Go into all the world and preach the gospel to all creation. Whoever believes and is baptized will be saved, but whoever does not believe will be condemned. And these signs will accompany those who believe: In my name they will drive out demons; they will speak in new tongues; they will pick up snakes with their hands; and when they drink deadly poison, it will not hurt them at all; they will place their hands on sick people, and they will get well.[2]*

Luke adds that the disciples were not to do anything until they had received the Holy Spirit, for which purpose Jesus asked them to wait in Jerusalem.[3]

---

[1] See Mark 16:1-14; Matthew 28:1-18; Luke 24:1-49; John 20:1-29; Acts 1:1-8.
[2] Mark 16:15-18. See also Matthew 28:18-20; Luke 24:47-48; Acts 1:8.
[3] See Luke 24:49.

Problems with the Story

An examination of the story of the resurrection and the events surrounding it reveals major problems that undermine their validity. These problems concern the women that came to the tomb of Jesus after the resurrection, Jesus' post resurrection appearances, the Pentecost, and Jesus' commission to his disciples to take the gospel to the world.

The Women at the Tomb

The gospels give different accounts concerning the visit of certain women to the tomb of Jesus on the day of the resurrection. Were there one, two, or three women? Who were the women? What happened at the tomb? Were there one, two, or many angels? Did the women tell the disciples of their experience, or did they scamper away in fear? Did Jesus allow the women to touch him, or did he forbid them from so doing? According to Mark's gospel,[4] three women – *Mary Magdalene, Mary the mother of James*, and *Salome* – went to the tomb. They discovered it empty, but angels informed them that Jesus had arisen and would precede his disciples to *Galilee* where they would see him. However, *bewildered and trembling with fear, the women ran away and said nothing to anyone, not even the disciples, about their experience.*[5] Jesus later appeared first to Mary Magdalene before appearing to two disciples alone, and then the eleven together.[6]

---

[4] See generally, Mark 16.
[5] Mark 16:8.
[6] Mark 16:9-19.

Luke reports that Mary Magdalene, Mary the mother of James, and *Joanna* went to the empty tomb and encountered angels who informed them that Jesus had arisen. Unlike in Mark, *the women went back and reported their experience to the disciples who thought they were speaking nonsense.* Peter then went to the empty tomb and left bewildered as to what might have happened.[7] However, in Matthew's account, only two women, *Mary Magdalene and 'the other Mary'*, had gone to the empty tomb. They discovered that a combination of a violent earthquake and *an angel* had moved away the huge stone covering it, after the angel had rendered the guards unconscious. The angel informed the women about the resurrection of Jesus and told them to relay the news to the disciples. As the women were going to tell the disciples, Jesus appeared to them. The women *'clasped his feet and worshiped him'*. Matthew then reports that the chief priests and the elders bribed the guards to lie that Jesus' disciples had come in the night to steal his body as they (the guards) slept.[8]

According to the gospel of John,[9] only *Mary Magdalene* went to the tomb. Discovering that the stone no longer covered the tomb, *she ran away and told Peter and the disciple 'whom the Lord loved' that, 'they have taken the Lord out of the tomb, and we don't know where they have put him!'*[10] Then, the two disciples, along with her ran to the tomb only to discover that it was empty. Peter and the other disciple

---

[7] See Luke 24:1-12.
[8] See Matthew 28:1-14.
[9] See generally, John 20.
[10] John 20:2.

went back home, while Mary stayed behind and cried. When she peered into the tomb, *she saw two angels dressed in white and complained to them that some people had taken her Lord away to an unknown destination.* At this point, Jesus appeared to her; but when Mary wanted to hold him, he restrained her by saying, *'Do not hold on to me, for I have not yet returned to the Father'.* He told her to go to his brothers and tell them that, 'I am returning to my Father and your Father, to my God and your God'. Mary then returned to the disciples and announced to them that she had seen the Lord, and relayed to them the message from Jesus.[11]

These discrepancies are significant because eyewitnesses would not forget or mix up such obvious and important details if the events had really occurred. These women, depicted as very close to Jesus and his disciples, would have been key figures in the early church whose members would know about their experiences. It is also doubtful why the women (or the woman) went to the tomb. While Mark and Luke report that they went to apply spices on Jesus' body (even though the body had already been treated with a mixture of myrrh and aloes, 'in accordance with Jewish burial customs'[12] before entombment), Matthew and John claim that they simply went to see the tomb.

The Post-resurrection Appearances

The gospels disagree on where Jesus instructed his disciples to await his appearance, and on where he eventually appeared to them after his

---

[11] John 20:17:18.
[12] See John 19:39-40.

resurrection. They also differ on the number of appearances. According to Mark and Matthew, Jesus appeared to the gathering of disciples in *Galilee*, the base of his ministry, having instructed them during his lifetime and after resurrection, to wait there for him.[13] However, in Luke, Jesus first appeared to two disciples on the road to *Emmaus – a village near Jerusalem. The two disciples after dining with Jesus at Emmaus returned to Jerusalem* and recounted their experience to others. Shortly after that, Jesus appeared to all the disciples in *Jerusalem* and ate with them. Jesus then told them to stay in Jerusalem and await the Holy Spirit.[14] Acts of the Apostles also reports that Jesus appeared to the gathering of the disciples in *Jerusalem*.[15] According to John's gospel, on the evening of the day of resurrection, Jesus appeared to the disciples and showed them his hands and side. Subsequently, he appeared to the doubting Thomas that was not with the other disciples at the original appearance. These appearances apparently took place in *Jerusalem*, despite the fact that Jesus had told the disciples (in Mark and Matthew) to await his appearance in *Galilee* and despite reports in those gospels that he did appear to them in *Galilee*.

However, a Galilee appearance on the same day of resurrection would be highly unlikely, given the distance of over 60 miles between that town and Jerusalem where the disciples were staying following the crucifixion. A Jerusalem appearance, though, would be inconsistent

---

[13] See Mark 16:7; Matthew 28:1-10.
[14] See Luke 24:14-49.
[15] See Acts 1:1-4.

with Jesus' express instructions. Although the Acts of Apostles and the gospel of John[16] claim that the resurrected Jesus stayed around for many weeks (forty days according to Acts) and appeared to the disciples many times, this claim is inconsistent with the accounts in the synoptic gospels. These clearly indicate that Jesus stayed only *one day* on earth after the resurrection and made only *one* appearance to the gathering of his disciples.[17] They also indicate that his appearance to the disciples and his ascension to heaven occurred on the day of resurrection. If these were the case, there could be no argument that Jesus appeared to the disciples in both Galilee and Jerusalem on different days. A Galilee appearance is also implausible on the ground that Jesus reportedly ascended into heaven from a location in Bethany, which was less than two miles from Jerusalem.[18] He could not have been with the disciples in Galilee and then returned with them to Bethany on the same day for the ascension.

Moreover, John 21, which narrates the other post-resurrection appearances, was not in the original gospel, which clearly ended at chapter 20. The stories in chapter 21 are obvious later additions to the gospel by redactors, apparently in order to add flesh to the claim in Acts, provide for a Galilee appearance in line with other gospels, and promote the primacy of Peter among the disciples. Observing that,

---

[16] See Acts 1:1-9; John 21.
[17] See Matthew 28:16-20; Luke 24; Mark 16:9-20.
[18] John 11:18.

'the gospels have too many inconsistences' in the post-resurrection narratives, the Oxford Dictionary of the Bible notes:

> *Mark ends 16:8 with the women running away in fear, and not telling anyone of what they had seen. This would seem to be an explanation by Mark to account for the story of the empty tomb not being part of the earliest kerygma.[19] Matthew expands on Mark, but its additions read like the story of the church and the Jews in the second half of the 1st Century rather than an account of the first Easter. Luke's narrative is historically questionable: he provides an impossible sequence of events for a single day [...][20]*

To confuse matters even more, Apostle Paul claims that the resurrected Christ appeared *first to Peter*, then to *the twelve* and then *to more than five hundred brothers and sisters.* Thereafter, he appeared *to James,* all the apostles, and finally *to Paul himself.[21]* Not only is this sequence of appearances different from the gospel accounts, the appearance to over five hundred brothers and sisters contradicts the Bible which states that at the time of the ascension of Jesus, the number of his followers was only one hundred and twenty.[22] Moreover, individual appearances to Peter and James were unreported in the gospels or Acts, while the purported appearance to Paul on the way to Damascus was not an appearance in the real sense of the term. Paul and his companions only observed a 'flashing light' from

---

[19] I.e., Christian preaching.
[20] WRF Browning (ed.) *Oxford Dictionary of the Bible* (Oxford University Press 2009) 313, 314.
[21] See 1 Corinthians 15:6-8.
[22] See Acts 1:15.

'heaven' accompanied by a voice claiming to be Jesus.[23] Neither he nor his fellow travellers saw anyone.

Nature of the Resurrected Jesus

The story concerning the nature of the resurrected Jesus is unrealistic. The gospels report that Jesus resurrected bodily and yet behaved not only as a material being, but also as a spirit. Materially, he had flesh and bones, bore the marks of crucifixion and ate food with his disciples.[24] As spirit, he went through closed doors and walls.[25] However, the spirit of a dead person would not remain with the body, and would not consume food or drinks meant for mortals. On the other hand, a soul cannot enter the spiritual realm if it remains in a body, and would therefore have no need or use for a material body. The gospel writers appeared so keen to affirm the Christian teaching of resurrection of the body, that they lost sight of these spiritual realities.

The Pentecost and the Holy Spirit

The Bible reports that before he ascended into heaven, Jesus promised to send the Holy Spirit to comfort his disciples and empower them for their mission of spreading the gospel. To this end, the gospel of Luke and Acts of the Apostles state that Jesus instructed the disciples to remain in Jerusalem until they receive the Holy Spirit.[26] The disciples apparently remained in Jerusalem, fearful and unable to preach the

---

[23] See Acts 9:3-9.
[24] See Luke 24:28-43; Acts 1:4.
[25] See Luke 24:36.
[26] Luke 24:49; Acts 1:4, 8.

gospel until the day of Pentecost when the Holy Spirit finally came upon them in the form of a rushing wind and tongues of fire. Filled with this Holy Spirit, the disciples began to speak in other tongues[27] and, led by Peter, they marched onto the streets and fearlessly preached the gospel of Jesus. Because they spoke in diverse tongues, diaspora Jews of all nationalities who had gathered in Jerusalem were able to understand them.[28]

For Peter, who spoke on behalf of the disciples, the outpouring and manifestation of the Holy Spirit was a fulfilment of the prophecy in Joel[29] that on the last days, God would pour his spirit on humans that would enable them to see visions, have dreams and do exploits. It was also for him, a fulfilment of prophecies by King David in the Psalms[30] that the body of Jesus would not remain in the grave or see decay, but would rise to heaven to sit at the right hand of God.[31] These supposed events have led to the celebration of that day in the church calendar, the emergence of the Pentecostal branch of Christianity, and the popularity of speaking in tongues. However, the Bible debunks the occurrence of the Pentecost and the events associated with it.

First, most of the gospels report that the disciples did not have to wait for the Holy Spirit; and two further suggest that they did not in fact receive it. Only the gospel of Luke and the Acts of the Apostles

---

[27] Act 2:1-4.
[28] See Acts 2:5-12.
[29] Joel 2:28-32.
[30] Psalm 16:8-11; 110:1.
[31] Acts 2:14-40.

(written by the same person) report that the disciples were to wait in Jerusalem in order to receive the Holy Spirit. However, according to the other gospels, Jesus, after his post-resurrection appearances to the disciples, immediately commissioned them to go into the world and preach the gospel, assuring them of his protection and giving them the ability to speak in new tongues and perform signs and wonders.[32] The power, which the disciples were supposed to receive on the day of Pentecost, according to Luke and Acts, had already been bestowed on them shortly after resurrection and prior to the ascension without any express or physical visitation of the Holy Spirit. In addition, according to the gospel of John, although the disciples did receive the Holy Spirit from Jesus, it was not in physical form and they did so shortly after resurrection, just before the ascension. According to John, after the resurrection, Jesus appeared to the disciples and, after wishing them peace, told them that he was sending them out as the Father had sent him. At this point, he *breathed on them and told them to receive the Holy Spirit*. He further told them that, any sins they forgive would be forgiven and those they did not forgive would not be forgiven.[33] By this account, the disciples did not need to huddle together anywhere in the wait for the Holy Spirit, and there were no tongues of fire.

Secondly, John refutes the claim in Luke and Acts that the disciples, after receiving the Holy Spirit, went about preaching the gospel. Instead, it reports that the disciples dispersed and went back to their

---

[32] See Mark 16:15-18; Matthew 28:16-20.
[33] See John 20:21-23.

previous occupations. Remarkably, Peter the chief disciple and some of his colleagues went back to fishing – an endeavour that received the appearance and blessing of Jesus. [34] Thus, rather than being fishers of men as Jesus had promised, Peter and his colleagues went back to being ordinary fishers. If Peter and his fellow disciples were out fishing, it would mean that they were not in the 'Upper Room'[35] to receive the Holy Spirit. It also would follow that Peter could not have made the rousing post-Pentecost speech attributed to him in Acts 2.[36]

Lastly, the story of the Pentecost relies on the mistaken belief that human beings are normally separated from God and do not have the divine spirit in them. This supposedly warrants a special dispensation by which the spirit of God would fall upon people. For Christians, this outpouring of the divine spirit is possible only through Jesus Christ. However, the divine spirit is always with us irrespective of religion. Since God is omnipresent, we (or more specifically our souls) are part of the places where the divine spirit inheres. Indeed, this divine spirit is responsible for human spiritual prowess and the tremendous inventions and innovations that have marked the progress of humankind. Since the divine spirit is natural to, and inherent in, our existence, there is no need to depend on the agency of any person in order to receive it.

---

[34] See John 21.
[35] This was the same room in which Jesus and his disciples reportedly ate the 'Last Supper.' See Luke 22:7-12.
[36] See Acts 2:14-40.

Therefore, the Spirit of God would be available to the disciples, just as the Bible says it was to other prominent Bible characters, and indeed the whole people of Israel. According to Isaiah, God promised to pour out water and stream on the dry and thirsty land of Israel, and to pour his spirit and blessings upon their descendants.[37] Ezekiel reports God as saying to the Israelites that, 'I will not hide My face from them any longer; for I will have poured out My Spirit on the house of Israel'.[38] The spirit of God was also on Prophet Isaiah, who declared that:

> *The Spirit of the Sovereign LORD is on me, because the LORD has anointed me to proclaim good news to the poor. He has sent me to bind up the broken-hearted, to proclaim freedom for the captives and release from darkness for the prisoners, to proclaim the year of the LORD's favour and the day of vengeance of our God, to comfort all who mourn* [...].[39]

If the people already had the Spirit of God, they would not need Jesus to obtain it; and, if the disciples of Jesus already had it, there would be no need for them to wait for the day of Pentecost in order to receive it. Seeing that the Pentecost claim appears to have been a ruse, did Jesus otherwise mandate his disciples to preach his message of salvation to the world as widely believed?

---

[37] Isaiah 44:3. See also Isaiah 11:2; 59:21.
[38] Ezekiel 39:29.
[39] Isaiah 61:1-2.

The Commission to take the Gospel to the World

The gospels all claim that Jesus commissioned his eleven surviving disciples to take his gospel not only to all parts of Israel but also to all corners of the world. In Matthew's account of the 'Great Commission', the resurrected Jesus allegedly told his disciples that:

> *All authority in heaven and on earth has been given to me.*
> *Therefore, go and make disciples of all nations, baptizing them*
> *in the name of the Father and of the Son and of the Holy Spirit,*
> *and teaching them to obey everything I have commanded you.*
> *And surely I am with you always, to the very end of the age.*[40]

The gospel of Mark adds that Jesus promised that those who believe and are baptised would be saved while those who do not would be damned. It adds that in the name of Jesus, the disciples could drive out demons, speak in new tongues, heal the sick, and would be impervious to deadly snakes and poisons.[41] Luke reports that, repentance and forgiveness of sins would be preached in the name of Jesus to all nations, beginning from Jerusalem;[42] while Acts states that Jesus asked his disciples to be his witnesses 'in Jerusalem, and in all Judea and Samaria, and to the ends of the earth'.[43] Although John was less explicit than the rest, its report in relation to this event was to a similar effect.[44]

---

[40] Matthew 28:18-20.

[41] Mark 16:15-18; see also Luke 24:46-47.
[42] See Luke 24:47.
[43] See Acts 1:8.
[44] See John 20:21-23.

In other places however, the Bible shows that there was no commissioning and that Jesus did not intend the gospel to get outside Israel. In his earlier statements and instructions, Jesus had made it clear that he did not wish to have his disciples or followers minister to Gentiles, his ministry and gospel being exclusively for the Jews. In Matthew 10: 5 – 7, Jesus ordered his disciples when he sent them on their first assignment not to 'go among the Gentiles or enter any town of the Samaritans', but 'to the lost sheep of Israel'. This injunction conforms to Jesus' other sayings. For example, when he was in Tyre and Sidon, a Canaanite woman had come begging him to heal her apparently demon-possessed daughter, a plea that irritated the disciples. After initially ignoring the woman, Jesus declared that, he was 'sent only to the lost sheep of Israel', and that 'it is not right to take the children's bread and toss it to the dogs'. When the women refused to be put off by these remarks and stated that, 'even the dogs eat the crumbs that fall from their masters' table', her daughter was healed due to her 'great faith'.[45] This was a clear indication to the disciples that the gospel of Jesus was not for the Gentiles.

On another occasion, Jesus assured his disciples that 'at the renewal of all things, when the Son of Man sits on his glorious throne, you who have followed me *will also sit on twelve thrones, judging the twelve tribes of Israel*'.[46] This clearly suggests to the disciples that their mission was limited to the twelve tribes of Israel. Paul confirmed

---

[45] Matthew 15: 21-28. See also Mark 7: 24-30.
[46] Matthew 19:22-29.

this in his letter to the Galatians. According to Paul, the disciples understood that he had been given the task of preaching the gospel to the gentiles 'just as Peter had been to the Jews':

> *For God, who was at work in the ministry of Peter as an apostle to the Jews, was also at work in my ministry as an apostle to the Gentiles. James, Peter and John, those reputed to be pillars, gave me and Barnabas the right hand of fellowship when they recognized the grace given to me. They agreed that we should go to the Gentiles, and they to the Jews.*[47]

Since the disciples were to preach the gospel only to Jews, and would be the judges of the twelve tribes of Israel, there is a direct contradiction between Jesus' instructions to his disciples when he was alive and his instructions to them after his resurrection.

The 'Great Commission' therefore appears to be a contrived afterthought. In fact, the gospel of Mark originally ended at chapter 16:8, with verses 9-20, which contain the Commission, being later additions by redactors. The New International Version of the Bible, for example, states after Mark 16 verse 8 that, 'the most reliable early manuscripts and other ancient witnesses do not have Mark 16: 9-20'. According to the explanatory notes in the Revised Standard Version of the Bible, there were two later attempts by redactors to give Mark's Gospel a better ending beyond verse 8 – the shorter ending and the longer ending. The longer ending was 'possibly written in the early second century and appended to the Gospel later in the second. These

---

[47] Galatians 2: 7-9 (emphasis added).

sentences borrow from the other Gospels and contain several apocryphal elements'.[48] Since Mark was the first gospel, and since Matthew and Luke appeared to use it (or its sources) extensively, it seems clear that the instruction to preach the gospel to the gentiles appeared first in the later gospels before its inclusion in Mark.

Jesus himself appeared to lay any argument about the alleged commission to rest by indicating that he did not expect the gospel to go beyond Israel before his second coming. While briefing the disciples before sending them out on their first mission in Israel, Jesus had warned them of the difficulties and persecutions that awaited them in the course of their ministry and of the societal upheavals imminent at the time. However, he assured them that, *'you will not finish going through the cities of Israel before the Son of Man comes'.*[49] Jesus reiterated this point when he gave the disciples the indicators that would herald his second coming. After recounting the signs and the tribulations and the manner of his appearance, he concluded by saying that, *'this generation will certainly not pass away until all these things have happened. Heaven and earth will pass away, but my words will never pass away'.*[50]

In the light of the foregoing, there appears to be no doubt that Jesus did not mean anyone to preach his gospel beyond Israel and that any

---

[48] *The New Oxford Annotated Bible, NRSV with the Apocrypha* (4[th]ed) (Oxford University Press 2010) 1824. See also BD Ehrman, *Whose Word Is It? The Story Behind Who Changed the New Testament and Why* (The Continuum International Publishing Group 2006) 65-69.
[49] Matthew 10:21-23, emphasis added.
[50] Matthew 24:34-35.

instruction to do so after his resurrection could not have come from him. The activities of the disciples and the manner in which the gospel got to the Gentiles clearly bear out this conclusion. Although the gospel of Mark claims that after the ascension of Jesus, the disciples preached the gospel everywhere',[51] and although church tradition holds that the disciples preached the gospel in many places outside Israel, there is little evidence that they ever ventured out of Israel. Instead, it was the seven brethren elected by the early church as welfare officers[52] and Paul, the former persecutor-in-chief of the Christians, and his associates,[53] that the Bible makes responsible for preaching the gospel outside Israel.[54]

Even when the early church in Israel scattered after the reported killing of Stephen, all the members except the eleven surviving disciples of Jesus remained in Israel.[55] In fact, so opposed were these to the preaching of the gospel to non-Jews that Peter would not minister to Cornelius of Caesarea, until 'the Lord' prevailed on him in a trance to do so.[56] Even then, the other disciples and Jewish Christians in Jerusalem were angry that Peter 'went to the house of

---

[51] See Mark 16:20.
[52] See Acts 6.
[53] Notably, Barnabas, Silas, Timothy and Titus, none of whom was a disciple of Jesus.
[54] Most of the evangelistic activities in the Acts of the Apostles were undertaken by these men; and most of the scripture in the New Testament are attributed or related to Paul. It is instructive that the first and only Christian martyr in the Bible was Stephen, one of the seven.
[55] See Acts 8, 11: 19-31; 15:2
[56] Acts 10.

uncircumcised men and ate with them'.[57] Peter had to defend his action by narrating the circumstances leading to it before these people relented, saying, 'So then, God has granted even the Gentiles repentance unto life'.[58]

After the Cornelius encounter, there is no record in the Bible that the apostles or other Jewish Christians embraced evangelism to Gentiles. On the contrary, when Paul and his gentile converts had succeeded in establishing churches abroad, the contribution of the Jerusalem Christians and disciples, was to attempt to derail the mission by going to the gentile converts and insisting that, unless they were circumcised according to the Law of Moses, they could not be saved.[59] The problem caused by this was so serious that it led to the convening of the first Church Council in Jerusalem between Jewish and gentile Christians. At the meeting, the Jewish Christians insisted that, 'the Gentiles must be circumcised and required to obey the Law of Moses'.[60] After extensive deliberations, the compromise reached was that circumcision should not be required of the gentile believers; but that they should only be required to abstain from foods sacrificed to idols, blood, meat of strangled animals, and sexual immorality'.[61] The logical conclusion to draw from the above analysis is that neither Jesus nor his disciples were in the least interested in, or inclined to spread, the gospel outside Israel. This is consistent with the fact that Jesus was

---

[57] Acts 11:1-3.
[58] Acts 10; 11.
[59] Acts 15:1.
[60] Acts 15: 5.
[61] Acts 15: 28-29.

a man fully committed to the laws, traditions, beliefs and religion of his people to the exclusion of others. The so-called commission to preach the gospel of salvation to the whole world appears, therefore, to be a sham.

Resurrections in Religious Mythology

The abundance of the tale of resurrection in religious mythology further damages the truthfulness and veracity of Jesus' resurrection story. In many ancient religions, the belief in the death and resurrection of gods or sons and daughters of gods for the purposes of saving or conferring other benefits to humanity appear as the archetypal hero's journey or descent to the underworld. These tales of dying and rising gods include those of Osiris of Egypt, Adonis of Phoenicia, and Attis of Phrygia.[62]

According to Egyptian mythology, Osiris was killed by Set, his evil brother, who put his body in a sealed coffin and dumped it into the sea. Set later dismembered the corpse into fourteen fragments. However, the goddess Isis – the sister and wife of Osiris – eventually recovered the body, and with the help of Ra, the sun god, restored it to life. Therefore, ancient Egyptians celebrated Osiris as the eternal Lord of the dead and underworld.[63]

---

[62] See JG Frazer, *Adonis Attis Osiris: Studies in the History of Oriental Religion* (London: Macmillan and Co. Ltd. 1906) 198-202.
[63] Ibid, 211-219. See also D Rosenberg, *World Mythology: An Anthology of the Great Myths and Epics* (McGraw Hill Companies Inc. 1994) 159-162.

In ancient Phoenician legend, Adonis allegedly spent part of the year in the underworld and the other part (about two-third) above the ground, with the times spent in both habitats corresponding to winter and spring/summer.[64] Thus, he died every year to the despair, wailings and lamentations of worshippers (especially women), but would resurrect and ascend into heaven to their joy.[65] Attis (Atys) was a Phrygian[66] vegetation and solar god related to Adonis. The cult of Attis included the celebration of his death and resurrection, which coincided with the beginning of spring and the vegetation season.[67]

Other gods who allegedly died and resurrected are Odin, the Norse god who hung himself on the World Tree to gain knowledge, Dionysus of Greece, Baal of Canaan, and Inanna or Dumuzi (Tammuz) of Mesopotamia.[68] In the Sumerian (Mesopotamian) legend, Inanna, the 'Queen of Heaven' descended naked into the underworld where the Queen of the Dead killed her and hung her body on a wall. She remained dead for *three days and three nights* before

---

[64] Phoenicia comprised parts of present day Lebanon, Syria and Northern Israel. Adonis (Tammuz in Babylonia) is a Hellenist name derived from 'Adon', a Canaanite god title meaning 'Lord' or 'Master'. The Hebrew, Adonai (my Lord) appears to be a derivative of this.

[65] See JG Frazer, supra n 62; Ezekiel 8:14.

[66] Phrygia would be in the northern part of today's Turkey.

[67] See *Encyclopaedia Britannica,* http://www.britannica.com/topic/Adonis-Greek-mythology;
http://www.britannica.com/topic/Attis.

[68] See the *Ancient History Encyclopaedia*, http://www.ancient.eu/Easter/. See also, J.G. Frazer, supra n 62, 3-8, 163-175; 211-219; D Rosenberg, supra n 63, 160-162; S Archaya, *The Christ Conspiracy: The Greatest Story Ever Sold* (Adventures Unlimited Press 2012) 107-125. See further *the Encyclopaedia Britannica*, http://www.britannica.com/topic/resurrection-religion.

her father, the god Enki, restored her to life.[69] In the Greco-Roman legend, the god-man Hercules, the son of the chief god Zeus, successfully descended into Hades to capture the ferocious three-headed dog Kerberos that guarded its gate.[70]

In many parts of the ancient world, the death and resurrection of gods were the peoples' way of explaining the transformation from darkness, and relative gloom and leanness of winter to the light, gaiety and productivity of spring and summer. Plants lose their leaves in autumn and remain unproductive and ill-looking throughout winter, only to come back to life in spring, regaining their leaves and vitality. In addition, spring (or its equivalent) is the planting season in many cultures, and thus a harbinger of life and bounty. These seasonal changes were associated with the state of the gods.[71] The ancients, it has been observed, 'pictured to themselves the growth and decay of vegetation, the birth and death of living creatures, as effects of the waxing or waning strength of divine beings, of gods and goddesses, who were born and died, who married and begot children, on the pattern of human life.'[72]

---

[69] See *The Ancient History Encyclopaedia,* http://www.ancient.eu/article/215/.

[70] See *The Ancient History Encyclopaedia,* http://www.ancient.eu/hercules/. See also GF Chesnut, *Images of Christ: An Introduction to Christology* (Seabury Press 1984) 132.

[71] See *The Ancient History Encyclopaedia*, http://www.ancient.eu/Cybele/; http://www.ancient.eu/venus/.

[72] JG Frazer, supra n. 114, ch. 2, 3.

Easter Festival

Ironically, the festival that purports to honour the resurrection of Jesus completely undermines it. Although Easter is the holiest and most important festival in the church calendar[73] and celebrated in commemoration of the resurrection of Jesus, it originally was a 'pagan' spring festival observed in honour of fertility gods, or in celebration of the onset of the spring season. The gods, whose dying and resurrection religions celebrate in the spring season, have already been highlighted in the preceding section. The word *Easter*, according to the Ancient History Encyclopaedia:

> [...] *comes from the Old English ēaster or ēastre, a festival of spring"*[74] *relating to the fertility goddess Eostre (Eastre or Ostara) who "owned an egg-laying rabbit or hare" symbolizing fertility and life.*[75] *The origin of the term 'Easter' is also linked to "the German 'Ostern', which comes from the Norse word "Eostrus", meaning 'spring'."*[76]

This relates to the Feast of Passover, the Jewish festival celebrated around the 14th day of the month of Nisan,[77] and with which Easter has a link. Although now generally associated with the 'deliverance' of Jewish firstborn sons in Egypt, the Passover appear originally to be

---

[73] See *The Catholic Encyclopaedia,*
http://www.newadvent.org/cathen/05224d.htm.

[74] See *The Encyclopaedia Britannica,*
http://www.britannica.com/EBchecked/topic/117239/church-year/67669/Easter.

[75] See *The Ancient History Encyclopaedia,* http://www.ancient.eu/Easter/. See also *The Catholic Encyclopaedia,* http://www.newadvent.org/cathen/05224d.htm.

[76] See *The Ancient History Encyclopaedia,* http://www.ancient.eu/Easter/.

[77] The month Nisan is the first month of the Jewish calendar and falls within March and April in the current Gregorian calendar.

a spring and agricultural festival, being only associated with the legend of deliverance from Egypt much later. According to the Jewish Encyclopaedia:

> The name פסח must be taken to be derived from that meaning of the root which designates the "skipping," "dancing" motions of a young lamb (Toy, in "Jour. Bib. Lit." 1897), only secondarily connoting "passing over" in the sense of "sparing." Pesaḥ, thus explained, is connected with pastoral life; it is the festival celebrated in early spring by the shepherds before setting out for the new pastures. [78]

Apparently, the disciples of Jesus continued to observe the Passover, as the latter had instructed them to do;[79] and had no specific observation of the death and resurrection. It was not until much later that, 'the Jewish feast was taken over into the Christian Easter celebration' with all its liturgical and ritualistic trappings, themes and connotations.[80] Thus, an erstwhile agricultural, seasonal or latterly, Jewish deliverance festival became transformed into a Christian festival commemorating the resurrection of Jesus.

Even after establishing Easter as a Christian festival, the church had no settled date for it, its observance in any year, just as the Feast of Passover, being dependent on the phases of the moon. Some Christian

---

[78] See *The Jewish Encyclopaedia*, http://www.jewishencyclopedia.com/articles/11933-passover. See also Joshua 5:10-12; 'Passover' in WRF Browning, supra n 20.
[79] See 1 Matthew 26: 17-30; Mark 14: 12-26; Luke 22:7-20; Corinthians 11:23-26. The mention of *Easter* in Acts 12:4 in the KJV is widely known as a substitution of the word *Pascha* (Passover) in the original Greek New Testament.
[80] See *The Catholic Encyclopaedia*, http://www.newadvent.org/cathen/05224d.htm.

sects, notably the Quartodecimans in Asia Minor, observed Easter in accordance with the timing of the Passover, irrespective of the day of the week in which it fell, while the others observed it on the subsequent Sunday. Eventually the church decided at the Council of Nicea in 325 CE that Christians universally should celebrate Easter on the first Sunday, following the full moon on or after the vernal equinox. This, apart from ensuring uniformity in the period of observance, aimed to detach Easter celebration from the Jewish Passover.[81]

The fertility symbolisms that usually accompany Easter, such as Easter eggs and bunnies, clearly indicate its pre-Christian origins. As the Ancient History Encyclopaedia observes, 'the egg symbolized perfection and wholeness in its natural state, and the rabbit was a symbol of fertility'.[82] The Easter lamb was a carry-over from the slaughter of lambs by Jews during the Feast of Passover, a connection made by John's gospel, when it states that the death of Jesus occurred when the Passover lambs were being slaughtered in the Temple.[83] The gospel also states that none of the bones of Jesus was broken, just as those of the Passover lambs are not broken.[84] Thus, in the same way Jewish offspring escaped death in Egypt during Passover, believers in

---

[81] See also *The Catholic Encyclopaedia*,
http://www.newadvent.org/cathen/05224d.htm. Despite this attempt, the festival is still observed at different times by the Eastern Orthodox and the Coptic churches; and the festival (Pascha) retains vestiges of the Passover.
[82] See *The Ancient History Encyclopaedia*, http://www.ancient.eu/Easter/.

[83] See John 19:14.
[84] See John 19:32, 33, 36.

Jesus would now escape condemnation and eternal death by the sacrifice of Jesus, the true Lamb of God.[85] This claim though is unfounded. As earlier discussed, different ancient religions had similar death and resurrection myths of their heroes or gods, and Easter was a pagan festival in honour of fertility gods, or the celebration of the spring season.

If Jesus did factually resurrect from death, the date of that event would not be a matter of conjecture, but would reside in the collective memory of his disciples and followers, as well as in the traditions of the early church. In that case, there would have been no need to copy and Christianise the pagan Easter or the Jewish Passover. It is because Easter has no connection to the alleged death and resurrection of Jesus that some Christian sects, such as the Restored Church of God,[86] the Jehovah's Witnesses[87] and the United Church of God, among others[88] do not observe it. Moreover, the association of Jesus with the Jewish Passover, and his depiction as the Passover Lamb, indicates that he could not be the Saviour of the world. The story of the slaughter of Egyptian firstborns and the sparing of their Israelite counterparts

---

[85] See http://www.britannica.com/EBchecked/topic/117239/church-year/67669/Easter. See also 1 Corinthians 5:7; John 1:29, 36; John 19:31, 36; *The Ancient History Encyclopaedia*, http://www.ancient.eu/Easter/.

[86] For the position of that church on Easter and its origins, see http://rcg.org/search.html?q=easter+and+easter+bunny.

[87] For the position of the Jehovah's Witnesses on this subject, see http://www.jw.org/en/bible-teachings/questions/bible-about-easter/.

[88] For the position of the United Church of God, see http://www.ucg.org/the-good-news/christians-who-dont-celebrate-easter-what-do-they-know.

during the Passover clearly denotes the actions of a national god, rather than a universal one.[89]

Sunday Worship

The day on which Christians venerate Jesus Christ provides the final evidence against the credibility of the resurrection story. Although Christians refer to Sunday as the 'Lord's Day' in apparent memory of this event, that day has little to do with the resurrection of Jesus. According to the Bible, the disciples of Jesus, just like their master, observed the Sabbath and lived in accordance with Jewish Law. There is no indication that they observed or celebrated Sunday or Easter in honour of Jesus. The adoption of Sunday as a day of Christian worship appears to have begun with Apostle Paul,[90] the erstwhile tormentor-in-chief of the early church, who insisted that the Christian order had supplanted the Jewish religious-cum-legal system. It is not surprising that gentile Christian converts in Asia Minor worshipped on Sunday, given that the worship of sun gods – Baal, Osiris, Mithra, Jupiter, etc. – was prevalent in the area. Apostle Paul, it must also be remembered, was born and grew up in Tarsus, a town in the region.

Beginning from about 300 CE, however, the prevailing ecclesiastical and secular authorities gradually began to make mandatory the observance of Sunday as the Christian Sabbath. First, Emperor Constantine, a sun worshipper and Christian convert, decreed Christianity as the state religion and Sunday as the day of worship.

---

[89] See Exodus 12:1-30.
[90] See Acts 20:7; 1 Corinthians 16:2.

Thereafter, the church christened Sunday as the Lord's Day and made failure to attend the Sunday Mass a venial sin. Subsequent edicts, decrees and practices ensured that the observance of the sun's day became entrenched around the Christian world.[91] The connection of Sunday to sun worship is the reason why many Christian sects refuse to worship on that day and still observe the Sabbath.[92] They believe the observance of Sunday as the Lord's Day is a corruption of Christianity by the devil.

However, contrary to claims that sun worship was a corruption of Christianity by the devil, there is enough evidence that the Bible itself identified Jesus Christ as a sun god. John's gospel calls Jesus the 'true light' whom the world did not recognise, while[93] Jesus referred to himself as 'the light of the world' that will eliminate darkness from his followers.[94] During the transfiguration, the Bible reports that the face of Jesus 'shone like the sun' and his clothes 'became as white as the light'.[95] Furthermore, in his vision, the writer of Revelation, states that, 'someone like the son of man' held seven stars in his hand, had eyes like blazing fire, and had a face 'like the sun shining in all its

---

[91] See
The Catholic Encyclopaedia, http://www.newadvent.org/cathen/14335a.htm. See also EG White, *The Spirit of Prophecy: The Great Controversy Between Christ and Satan,* Vol. IV, 1969 (Washington: Review and Herald Publishing Association 1969) 39-65.
[92] For a list of these sects or denominations, see http://www.the-ten-commandments.org/sabbathkeepingchurches.html.
[93] John 1:9.
[94] John 8:12.
[95] Matthew 17:2; Mark 9:3.

brilliance'.[96] He also states that Jesus was 'the bright morning star'.[97] These epithets are not merely figurative or metaphorical. The Catholic Encyclopaedia reports that, for a long time, sun worship was rampant within the walls of the Vatican Basilica.[98] Moreover, Church buildings, consistent with 'pagan' practice, traditionally aligned with the rising sun, and Christians prayed while facing east.[99]

That early Christians worshipped the sun is not as remarkable as it might seem if we remember that the worship of the sun and the moon was prevalent among ancient peoples from whose ranks the gentile Christians emerged, and even among ancient Israelites. The Mosaic Law would not proscribe the worship of the sun and other heavenly bodies and prescribe the death penalty for it, were the practice uncommon.[100] As narrated in the Bible's Old Testament, the religious reforms of King Josiah included doing away with priests 'who burned incense to Baal, to the sun and moon, to the constellations and to all the starry hosts'.[101] However, despite the efforts of Josiah, sun worship remained prevalent throughout Israel among kings, government officials, priests, prophets and the ordinary people, as indicated in the lamentations of Prophets Jeremiah and Ezekiel.[102]

---

[96] Revelation 1:14, 16.
[97] Revelation 22:16.
[98] See The Ten Commandments, http://www.newadvent.org/cathen/02084a.htm.
[99] See *The Catholic Encyclopaedia*,
http://www.newadvent.org/cathen/01362a.htm.
[100] See Deuteronomy 4:19; 17:2-3.
[101] See 2 Kings 23:5.
[102] Jeremiah 8:1-2; Ezekiel 8.

Although the penchant of the Israelites to worship the sun apparently riled Yahweh, the worshippers appeared actually to identify him with the sun. For example, Psalm 84:11 calls Yahweh 'a sun and shield', and Psalm 104:1-4 describes him in terms clearly evocative of solar characteristics. In addition, Prophet Malachi observed that for those who fear the name of Yahweh, 'the Sun of Righteousness shall arise, with healing on its wings'.[103] In any event, it is very clear from the Bible that there is little difference between Yahweh and the sun gods, Baal, and El.[104]

The inevitable conclusion to draw from all the evidence is that, although key to the claim that Jesus is the Christ, the resurrection story, rather than being a narration of facts, merely reflects Christian belief and mythology akin to those about some other gods and heroes extant at the time the gospel stories were constructed.[105] It therefore seems that the fear of Paul – that if Jesus did not resurrect from the dead, the preaching and faith of Christians would be useless, and they would be bearers of false witness about God – has been realised. Unless of course, Jesus ascended to heaven.

---

[103] Malachi 4:2.

[104] See LE Modeme, *Fantasy of Salvation* (Ameze Resources Ltd. 2019).

[105] See EP Sanders, *The Historical Figure of Jesus* (London: Penguin Books 1995) 276-281. Although sympathetic to the gospel narratives, the author could not ignore many of these problems.

CHAPTER 10

DID JESUS ASCEND TO HEAVEN?

He ascended into heaven, and sits at the right hand of God the Father Almighty; from thence, he shall come to judge the quick and the dead. – The Apostles Creed

Clearly, if there was no resurrection, there could not have been any ascension either. However, the ascension of Jesus was supposed to mark the culmination of his life and ministry on earth and the hope of his eventual return. This is because, having gone to heaven, he would prepare a heavenly home to which he would take his followers upon his second coming. Therefore, unless Jesus did ascend to heaven, there would be no possibility of his coming back since he would, on death (assuming he lived and died), have gone the way of ordinary mortals. In that case, any expectation of a final judgment and heavenly reward for believers would be completely nugatory. Moreover, if Jesus did not ascend to heaven, the claim that he was God or the only Son of God would be unsustainable, especially if other religions have similar ascension claims.

The Ascension Story

Luke's gospel reports that the risen Jesus led his disciples to the vicinity of Bethany, and after he had blessed them, 'was taken up into heaven'.[1] According to Acts, after the risen Jesus had appeared to his disciples in Jerusalem over a period of forty days, and after commissioning them to go and preach the gospel, 'he was taken up before their very eyes, and a cloud hid him from their sight'. As the disciples were looking up the sky in astonishment, two angels appeared and assured them that, 'this same Jesus, who has been taken from you into heaven, will come back in the same way you have seen him go into heaven'.[2] Mark's gospel adds that, having ascended into heaven, Jesus 'sat at the right hand of God',[3] a claim repeated in 1 Peter 3:22. There is no account of the ascension in the gospels of Matthew and John. The claims regarding the ascension of Jesus aligns with statements earlier attributed to Jesus that he would ascend to heaven,[4] and claims in the Epistles of Paul affirming the ascension.[5] However, is this tale factual?

Did Jesus Ascend to Heaven?

A close examination reveals that the ascension story has no basis in reality, but rests on religious beliefs and mythology reminiscent of those in many ancient cultures and religions around the world. In the first place, the story is entirely hearsay, with only the gospel of Luke

---

[1] See Luke 24:50-52.
[2] See Acts 1:9-11.
[3] See Mark 16:19.
[4] See John 6:63; 20:17.
[5] See Ephesians 4:8-10; Timothy 3:16.

and the Acts of Apostles (written by the same author) originally carrying it. The account in Mark's gospel was a later addition and an apparent attempt by Bible writers to harmonise it with Luke's account. As was earlier observed, the gospel of Mark ended originally at chapter 16, verse 8; but the story of the post-resurrection appearances and ascension appear in the added verses 9-20. Since Mark's post-resurrection and ascension stories are fictitious, and since Mark was the first gospel, the contents of which the author of Luke must have been aware,[6] it follows that Luke's post-resurrection appearance and ascension stories were similarly contrived. Considering how remarkable and unforgettable an observed physical ascension to heaven would be to the observers, it is inconceivable that the disciples who witnessed it, and the early Christians to whom they must have narrated it, would have forgotten about it. This being the case, it is very unlikely that the writers of the gospels of Mark, Matthew and John would forget or fail to include the event in their narratives. The fact that the ascension account appeared only in Luke (a self-confessed hearsay gospel), and was repeated in Acts by the same author, is indicative of unreality.

Second, there is a contradiction between Luke and Acts of the Apostles on the day of the ascension. According to Luke (and echoed in Mark), the ascension took place in Bethany on the same day of the resurrection.[7] However, Acts reports that it happened not less than

---

[6] See Luke 1:1-4.
[7] See Luke 24:50-51; Mark 16:18-19.

forty days after the resurrection by the Mount of Olives.[8] If the ascension did take place, the exact date and time of its occurrence would fix permanently in the memory of the observers and the early Christians. Although Mount Olives and Bethany could refer to the same location, the discrepancy between one day and forty days in the accounts is inexplicable considering that the same hand apparently wrote both accounts.

Third, the claim in Mark and 1 Peter that Jesus 'sat at the right hand of God' was clearly not factual but reflects Christian belief and teaching. The gospels report that before his death, Jesus told his interrogators that they 'will see the Son of Man sitting at the right hand of the Mighty One and coming on the clouds of heaven'.[9] Jesus had, on another occasion, related Psalm 110:1 apparently in reference to himself: 'The LORD says to my Lord, "Sit at my right hand until I make your enemies a footstool for your feet". Similarly, Ephesians 1:19-21 proclaims that God raised Jesus from the dead 'and seated him at his right hand in the heavenly realms, far above all rule and authority, power and dominion, and every name that is invoked, not only in the present age but also in the one to come'.[10]

This belief, reiterated in the Apostles' Creed, suggests a specially privileged position for Jesus in relation to God. In Mark 10:37, James

---

[8] See Acts 1:9-12.
[9] See Mark 14:62; Matthew 26:64; Luke 22:69.
[10] See also Romans 8:34 for a similar claim.

and John, the sons of Zebedee, apparently desired this kind of privilege by requesting that they be allowed to sit on the right and left hands of Jesus in his glory. If Jesus had ascended into heaven, the disciples who reportedly observed it would not have been able, from the ground, to see the interiors of heaven and Jesus sitting down beside God. Indeed, the Acts of Apostles reports that as Jesus was ascending into heaven, and as the disciples watched, 'a cloud hid him from their sight'. If a cloud had hidden the ascending Jesus from the sight of the watching disciples, how could they have seen him sitting down on the right hand of God? It is in a similar manner that Acts 7:55-56 reports that Stephen, while filled with the Holy Spirit, saw Jesus standing (not sitting) in heaven by the right hand of God – a claim that is obviously not factual.

Fourth, the ascension curiously took place in relative secrecy in the presence only of the disciples. Given that Jesus apparently meant to change Israel and the world with his ministry; given the hostility and unbelief that attended this attempt; and given the need to convince the people of his status as the messiah, one would expect that many people, including doubters and unbelievers, would witness the ascension and post-resurrection appearances. Jesus ascending to heaven before only his disciples does little in aid of his gospel. This is because even the disciples of Jesus, despite their long and close association with him, doubted that he had resurrected, prompting Jesus to convince them by showing his crucifixion scars and eating with them. If Jesus needed to convince his best fans of his resurrection by appearing to them; if he needed to convince them about his return to heaven by ascending in their presence, it is strange that he did not see the need to appear to members of the public, or to make a publicly observable ascension.

Fifth, Jesus reportedly resurrected and ascended into heaven with the same body with which he had lived on earth and which had earlier eaten food, bore nail scars and been touched by the disciples. If the risen Jesus was still bones, flesh and blood, he could not have ascended into heaven. Given that Jesus did not come down to the earth with his heavenly body but had to be born and raised from infancy to adulthood in a human body, why would he need to ascend to heaven with his earthly body?

Finally, there is no record of the ascension anywhere, other than in the gospel of Luke and Acts of Apostles. If the ascension took place, it is inconceivable that the disciples who witnessed would not make a note of it. The narratives were also neither contemporaneous with the relevant events nor written by contemporaries of Jesus. Instead, unidentified apologists wrote them many decades after the purported events. The purpose of the ascension story, as well as the other gospel stories, is to glorify Jesus and not necessarily to report facts. According to John's gospel, 20:31, the gospels 'are written that you may believe that Jesus is the Messiah, the Son of God, and that by believing you may have life in his name'.

Ascension in Religions and Mythology

Although Jesus reportedly claimed that, 'no one has ever gone into heaven except the one who came from heaven – the Son of man',[11] this would seem not to be the case as there are tales of ascension in some other religions, including Judaism and Islam. According to the Bible, Enoch and Elijah ascended alive into heaven a long time before Jesus. In the words of Genesis 5:24, 'Enoch walked faithfully with God; then he was no more, because God took him away'. Amplifying this claim, Hebrews 11:5 states that Enoch was taken away alive from earth and into heaven and immortality; and the apocryphal Book of Enoch reports the ascended Enoch as giving a vivid description of heaven.[12] In 2 Kings 2:11, Elijah was reportedly taken into heaven in a whirlwind as his apprentice Elisha watched. This Elijah (along with Moses) was later to appear from heaven and stand beside Jesus during his transfiguration.[13] There was no suggestion in the Bible that Enoch or Elijah was, by virtue of their ascension into heaven, messiahs.[14]

In ancient Greco-Roman religion, the god Heracles/Hercules allegedly ascended into heaven from Mount Oiti (Oeta).[15] In Sumerian religious mythology, Adapa (Adamu) – the son of the god Ea (or Enki)

---

[11] See John 3:13.

[12] See Book of Enoch (books 1 – to 3, http://book-ofenoch.com/; and Chapter 21.

[13] See Matthew 17:17; Luke 9:28-36; Mark 9:2-13.

[14] The Ascension of Isaiah, an apocryphal book, also reports that Prophet Isaiah ascended into heaven. See *The Jewish Encyclopaedia*, http://www.jewishencyclopedia.com/articles/8237-isaiah-ascension.

[15] See http://www.britannica.com/EBchecked/topic/262467/Heracles. See also D Rosenberg, *World Mythology: An Anthology of the Great Myths and Epics* (McGraw Hill Companies Inc. 1994) 30-31.

– temporarily ascended into heaven to meet the father god, Anu, who was unhappy about his breaking of the wings of the South Wind, causing the wind to stop blowing.[16] In the same tradition, Etana, the king of Kish allegedly ascended into heaven on the giant wings of an eagle.[17] Further, according to Roman legend, Romulus, one of the legendary twin brothers believed to have founded Rome, ascended into heaven in a whirlwind and became a god.[18] Finally, Moslems believe that Prophet Mohammed ascended to heaven while still alive.[19] The legend of the ascension of Jesus is not different from these and others like them.

If Jesus did not ascend to heaven, it would mean that he cannot return to the world to take his followers to heaven as he allegedly promised. Accordingly, the last vestige of hope in the reality of the gospel stories, or the claim that Jesus might be the messiah, evaporates. It remains to be seen whether the Bible provides any significant information about the person and life of Jesus Christ, and whether secular sources confirm any aspect of the gospel story.

---

[16] See the *Encyclopaedia Britannica,*
http://www.britannica.com/EBchecked/topic/5254/Adapa.
[17] See *The* Ancient History Encyclopaedia, http://www.ancient.eu/article/224/.
[18] See *The Ancient History Encyclopaedia,*
http://www.ancient.eu/Romulus_and_Remus/. See also, in general, D Rosenberg, *World Mythology: An Anthology of the Great Myths and Epics* (McGraw Hill Companies Inc. 1994); GF Chesnut, *Images of Christ: An Introduction to Christology* (Seabury Press 1984) 89.
[19] See Chapter 7.

CHAPTER 11

DID JESUS HAVE A PERSONALITY?

There is no trustworthy tradition concerning the bodily appearance of Jesus, but this is not needed in order to obtain a picture of His character [...] Some call Him a fanatic, others make Him a socialist, others again an anarchist, while many call Him a dreamer, a mystic, an Essene. – The Catholic Encyclopaedia[1]

According to the Bible, the first public appearance of Jesus was at the age of twelve when he dodged his family and went into the temple to engage learned scribes in scriptural discourse with great wisdom.[2] After that incident, Jesus' next appearance was as an adult of about 30 years at his baptism.[3] From there, he went into the wilderness where he faced temptation from the Devil. Having overcome the temptations,[4] Jesus chose some disciples and began his ministry.[5] In the course of his ministry, Jesus preached in many places and did many amazing miracles. He drew many followers and attracted numerous admirers and enemies. The ministry

---

[1] http://www.newadvent.org/cathen/08382a.htm.
[2] See Luke 2:39-52.
[3] See Matthew 3:13-17 and Chapter 4.
[4] See Chapter 5.
[5] See Chapter 6.

lasted between one and three years,[6] after which Jesus was crucified and buried.[7] He then resurrected and shortly afterwards ascended into heaven.[8] Given the above antecedents, the personal appearance and characteristics of Jesus should not be conjectural but matters of common knowledge among members of his family, friends, peers and the wider Jewish community. So, what did Jesus, the god-man of the gospels, look like? What does the Bible say about his personal life and character?

Physical Appearance

The common image of Jesus is that of a handsome and majestic (usually Caucasian-looking) man with long flowing hair and a well-trimmed beard wearing long fine robes. However, these images are fictional and speculative since there is no physical description of Jesus in the Bible, and no contemporary description or images of him existed or exist. One thing though is certain: If Jesus lived, he would not have looked like the images commonly depicted in pictures and movies. Instead, he would have been much darker and similar in appearance to ordinary men of ancient Near East, Egypt and Ethiopia, were he was supposedly born and raised. In fact, the Bible books of Revelation and Daniel describe the 'Son of Man' and the 'Ancient of Days' (titles given to Jesus) as having woollen white hair and the

---

[6] Depending on which gospel account one takes: the synoptic or John's.
[7] See Chapter 8.
[8] See Chapters 9 and 10.

colour of 'bronze glowing in a furnace.'[9] These descriptions are decidedly non-Caucasian.

In addition, Jesus would not have had a well-trimmed beard, since it was against the law and custom of the Jews for men to shave or trim their beards, except in mourning or penance.[10] He would also not have had long flowing hair since it was similarly against Jewish law and custom. That was why Nazarites (which Jesus was not)[11] left their hair uncut and in locks as a sign of self-deprecation. In fact, long hair for Jewish men was unnatural and humiliating.[12] Since Jesus was a Rabbi, he would have kept these rules scrupulously. Moreover, since he was supposedly a peasant carpenter, and condemned the accumulation of wealth and earthly belongings, it was unlikely that he would have moved about adorned in fine robes.

There is however, a claim in Christian circles[13] that a description of Jesus appears in Isaiah 53:2, as follows:

> *He grew up before him like a tender shoot, and like a root out of dry ground. He had no beauty or majesty to attract us to him, nothing in his appearance that we should desire him. He*

---

[9] Revelation 1:15; Daniel 7:9-10.

[10] See Leviticus 19:27, 21:5; Jeremiah 9:25; 2 Samuel 10:15, 20:9; Job 1:20; Ezekiel 5:1.

[11] Nazarites took a vow to live an ascetic life, abstain from alcohol and other intoxicants, and refrain from touching corpses. Biblical examples are Samson (Judges 13:7) and Samuel (1 Samuel 1:1-11), and probably John the Baptist (see Mark 1:4-6; Matthew 3:4-6). In any event, Jesus never lived an ascetic life. He ate well, drank wine liberally and fasted only on one occasion – before his 'temptation', for which see Chapter 4. He also touched a corpse, on at least one occasion (see Mark 5: 41-43).

[12] See 1 Corinthians 11:14.

[13] See e.g. Acts 8: 30 – 35.

was despised and rejected by men, a man of sorrows, and familiar with suffering. Like one from whom men hide their faces he was despised, and we esteemed him not.

If this were a description of Jesus, it would suggest that he did not look like the man depicted in popular imagery. However, there is little to suggest that this passage refers to Jesus. Rather, it could have been about any of a number of major Old Testament characters, who were regarded as 'Servants of the Lord', including Moses, Jeremiah, King Josiah, and King Jehoiachin, among others.[14] So why are there no physical descriptions of Jesus in the Bible even though the gospels strive to show that, though divine, he was fully human, had a human family, and lived and worked among his people for about thirty-three years? Given the belief by many early Christians that Jesus' humanity was merely illusory and the fact that the gospels strive to counter this,[15] the absence of a physical description of Jesus is telling. This might be for two reasons.

The first is that apparently none of the writers of the gospels and the New Testament books knew or saw Jesus.[16] Paul, the most prolific New Testament writer, did not appear to have seen Jesus either even though both were supposed to be contemporaries. The other New Testament letters – James, John, Jude and Peter – as well as the book

---

[14] See the notes on Isaiah 52 and 53 in The *New Oxford Annotated Bible* (with Apocrypha) (NRSV) (4[th]ed, Oxford University Press 2010) 1038-1040.

[15] Gnosticism and Docetism held that Jesus never came in the flesh but was only divine. This belief was widespread amongst early Christians. See the *Catholic Encyclopaedia,* http://www.newadvent.org/cathen/06592a.htm; http://www.newadvent.org/cathen/05070c.htm.

[16] See Chapter 12.

of Revelation – were not the writings of the brother or apostles of Jesus as church tradition holds but those of undisclosed Christian apologists.[17] Although the church attributes the authorship of the Acts of the Apostles and Luke's Gospel, to Luke, the writer of that book is also unknown.[18] Since therefore, the relevant Bible writers have apparently not seen Jesus, it is not surprising that they could not describe him. The gospel of Mark begins its account of the life and times of Jesus with his adult baptism and the commencement of his ministry, saying nothing about how he was born, or what he looked like. John's gospel, the authorship of which is ascribed to the beloved disciple of Jesus, began with a declaration of the pre-existence of Jesus and how 'The Word' was made flesh'.[19] For John, as well as Mark, Jesus might have suddenly dropped straight down from the sky as a grown man just in time to commence his ministry. For a writer who was supposed to have grown up in the same locality as Jesus, and who was supposed to have been Jesus' closest disciple, this is strange.

The second reason why there is no information on the physical appearance of Jesus might be that no oral tradition existed among the earliest Christians about this. If such a tradition existed, descriptions or depictions of Jesus could have appeared in contemporary literature, carvings, drawings or sculptures. However, no such things exist or

---

[17] See *The New Oxford Annotated Bible, New Oxford Annotated Bible, NRSV with the Apocrypha* (4[th]ed) (Oxford University Press 2010) - Introductions to James, John, Jude and Peter and revelations.

[18] Ibid - Introductions to Luke's gospel and the Acts of the Apostles. See also BD Ehrman, *Whose word Is It? The Story behind who changed the New Testament and Why* (The Continuum International Publishing Group 2006).

[19] John 1:1-2, 14.

appear to have existed. If any oral tradition existed on the physical appearance of Jesus, such a tradition would, most likely have found its way into some, at least, of the New Testament writings. The Catholic Encyclopaedia admits that, 'there is no trustworthy tradition concerning the bodily appearance of Jesus', although it claims that this is not necessary in order to obtain a picture of his character.[20] However, if Jesus had lived, it is improbable that a tradition about his appearance would not exist.

Could it be that early Christians did not really care about the physical personality of Jesus? This is unlikely since from early Christian times, supposed images and icons of Jesus adorned churches, cathedrals and church paintings. In fact, Christians so venerated these icons and images that the Iconoclast Council of 754 CE felt the need to rule against the act on the ground of idolatry. However, ordinary use of the icons received the blessings of the seventh Ecumenical Council of 784 CE. Inasmuch as the Reformation heralded the abandonment of images and icons by the Protestants, the Catholics still use them, while the Eastern Orthodox Churches see their use as an essential part of worship. Considering that the doctrine of divine incarnation was an attempt partly to humanise and personalise God, the use of images and icons of Jesus is not surprising. These icons and images were, however, only conjectures of what Jesus might have looked like.

---

[20] http://www.newadvent.org/cathen/08382a.htm.

Attempts to Describe Jesus

The absence of biblical or traditional information has, however, not stopped people from coming up with physical descriptions of Jesus. One prominent example of these was the 'Shroud of Turin', which appeared in the 14th Century. This was a piece of cloth in which the body of Jesus was supposedly wrapped after his death. Although the Catholic Church had originally claimed that the shroud showed the authentic facial impression of Jesus, it has since admitted – in the face of the emergence of many other 'authentic' shrouds[21] – that the Shroud of Turin was not, in fact, the burial cloth of Jesus but a painting by an artist.

Another prominent 'description' of Jesus was that given in 1421 by a certain Publius Lentulus, a purported governor of Judea before the reign of Pontius Pilate. In the letter supposedly sent to the Roman Senate, Publius Lentulus provided a description of Jesus as follows:

> *He is a man of medium size; he has a venerable aspect, and his beholders can both fear and love . His hair is of the colour of the ripe hazelnut, straight down to the ears, but below the ears wavy and curled, with a bluish and bright reflection, flowing over his shoulders. It is parted in two on the top of the head, after the pattern of the Nazarenes. His brow is smooth and vary cheerful with a face without wrinkle or spot, embellished by a slightly reddish complexion. His nose and mouth are faultless. His beard is abundant, of the colour of his hair, not long, but divided at the chin. His aspect is simple and mature, his eyes are changeable and bright. He is terrible in his reprimands, sweet and amiable in his admonitions,*

---

[21] See
The Catholic Encyclopaedia, http://www.newadvent.org/cathen/13762a.htm.

cheerful without loss of gravity. He was never known to laugh, but often to weep. His stature is straight, his hands and arms beautiful to behold. His conversation is grave, infrequent, and modest. He is the most beautiful among the children of men.

The Church has, however, dismissed the so-called Publius Lentulus as fictitious and the letter as a fabrication designed to match the existing portraits of Jesus in church circles.[22]

There was also a claim that Pontius Pilate provided a description of Jesus. In a letter he purportedly wrote to Emperor Tiberius concerning Jesus, he allegedly painted a picture of Jesus' personality, appearance and character. The letter reads as follows:

To Tiberius Caesar:

A young man appeared in Galilee preaching with humble unction, a new law in the Name of the God that had sent Him. At first, I was apprehensive that His design was to stir up the people against the Romans, but my fears were soon dispelled. Jesus of Nazareth spoke rather as a friend of the Romans than of the Jews. One day I observed in the midst of a group of people a young man who was leaning against a tree, calmly addressing the multitude. I was told it was Jesus. This I could easily have suspected so great was the difference between Him and those who were listening to. His golden colored hair and beard gave to his appearance a celestial aspect. He appeared to be about 30 years of age. Never have I seen a sweeter or more serene countenance. What a contrast between Him and His bearers with their black beards and tawny complexions! Unwilling to interrupt Him by my presence, I continued my walk but signified to my secretary to join the group and listen.

---

[22] See
The Catholic Encyclopaedia, http://www.newadvent.org/cathen/09154a.htm.

Later, my secretary reported that never had he seen in the works of all the philosophers anything that compared to the teachings of Jesus. He told me that Jesus was neither seditious nor rebellious, so we extended to Him our protection. He was at liberty to act, to speak, to assemble and to address the people. This unlimited freedom provoked the Jews – not the poor but the rich and powerful.

Later, I wrote to Jesus requesting an interview with Him at the Praetorium. He came. When the Nazarene made His appearance I was having my morning walk and as I faced Him my feet seemed fastened with an iron hand to the marble pavement and I trembled in every limb as a guilty culprit, though he was calm. For some time I stood admiring this extraordinary Man. There was nothing in Him that was repelling, nor in His character, yet I felt awed in His presence. I told Him that there was a magnetic simplicity about Him and His personality that elevated Him far above the philosophers and teachers of His day.

Now, Noble Sovereign, these are the facts concerning Jesus of Nazareth and I have taken the time to write you in detail concerning these matters. I say that such a man who could convert water into wine, change death into life, disease into health; calm the stormy seas, is not guilty of any criminal offense and as others have said, we must agree – truly this is the Son of God.

Your most obedient servant,

Pontius Pilate.

This purported letter by Pilate concerning Jesus is obviously a fabrication designed to put in the pen of Pilate statements concerning the portrayal of Jesus in the gospels and church tradition. As noted by the Catholic Encyclopaedia, there was a considerable body of forged 'apocryphal Pilate literature', which attempted to put words into the mouth of Pilate in confirmation of the gospel story of Jesus. These writings usually exaggerate 'Pilate's weak defence of Jesus into strong sympathy and practical belief in His divinity'.[23] The purported letter to Tiberius was one such document. There is no record in the gospels, church or Roman historical records that Pontius Pilate ever saw or met Jesus before the trial. If Pontius Pilate had met Jesus, and was so awe-struck and convinced that he was the divine son of God, he could not have condemned him to crucifixion as the gospels claim. He could also not have mocked Jesus or ordered his scourging prior to execution. Indeed, he would have found it impossible to explain to the Emperor that he had executed such a man and released a murderous insurrectionist in the person of Barabbas in his stead.

Life and Character

In addition to the absence of a physical description of Jesus, the Bible says nothing about his personal life. Nobody had or has any idea what he did between infancy and 12 years and between 12 and 30 years; where he was; what his character was; whether he was married or single; etc. Although it is widely believed that Jesus was a carpenter like Joseph his adoptive father, this is a mere conjecture. Accordingly, claims abound in legend and different writings, including non-canonical gospels, attributing different characteristics to him and

---

[23] See http://www.newadvent.org/cathen/01601a.htm#III2.

placing him in different places around the world.[24] Thus, although Jesus assumedly lived a perfect and sin-free life,[25] there are no facts to back up this supposition, especially given that he went to John the Baptist for a baptism of repentance and forgiveness.[26] Indeed, far from being perfect, many of the teachings and utterances credited to Jesus in the gospels suggest human fallibilities, while some depict unpleasant characteristics.[27]

The absence of specific information on the person and character of Jesus has led to the emergence in Christology of Jesus of different characters depending on who was writing and the image they wish to project.[28] Observing that different investigators have arrived at completely different conclusions about Jesus, the Catholic Encyclopaedia notes that, 'some call Him a fanatic, others make Him a socialist, others again an anarchist, while many call Him a dreamer, a mystic, an Essene'.[29] It also observes that:

> *Some consider Jesus an ascetic, others an aesthete; some emphasize His suffering, others His joyfulness; some identify Him with ecclesiasticism, others with humanism; some recognize in Him the prophetic picture of the Old Testament*

---

[24] For an account of some of these, see JB Lumpkin, *The Life of Saint Issa, Best of the Sons of Man: The Missing Years of Jesus and His Travels in the East* (Fifth Estate 2012); AT Bradford, *The Jesus Discovery: Another Look at Christ's Missing Years* (Templehouse 2010); https://www.huffingtonpost.com/paul-davids/jesus-lost-years-may-fina_b_179513.html?guccounter=1.

[25] See e.g., Hebrews 4:15; 2 Corinthians 5:21; 1 John 3:5; Peter 2:22.

[26] See Chapter 4.

[27] For an analyses of some of these, see LE Modeme, Fantasy of Salvation (Ameze Resources Ltd. 2019).

[28] For more details, see Chapter 12.

[29] *The Catholic Encyclopaedia*, http://www.newadvent.org/cathen/08382a.htm.

and the monastic of the New, others see in Him only gladness and poetry.[30]

Since all that is 'known' about Jesus' person and character through the Bible are mere conjectures, can we glean any useful information about him and his life from history?

---

[30] Ibid.

CHAPTER 12

DOES HISTORY SAY ANYTHING ABOUT JESUS CHRIST?

Then they were all amazed, so that they questioned among themselves, saying, "What is this? What new doctrine is this? For with authority, He commands even the unclean spirits, and they obey Him". And immediately His fame spread throughout all the region around Galilee. – Mark 1: 27-28

To the believer, the gospels, supported by the rest of the New Testament, furnish incontrovertible historical evidence of the life, times and ministry of Jesus. Since they portray Jesus as a famous person who lived, worked, died, and resurrected at a certain period in history, in a certain part of the world before ascending to heaven, these events should be historically verifiable. Moreover, since these are essential to Christ's salvific mission, history should attest to them, otherwise his entire story would be little more than a religious fable. Although much time, ink and paper of several authors have gone into the issue, it is necessary here to examine claims concerning the historicity of Jesus Christ.

Are the Gospels History?

As evident from the discussions so far, and as noted in the preceding chapter, the stories about the life, mission, passion, resurrection and ascension of Jesus are contained only in the gospels and the Acts of the Apostles. However, contrary to popular belief and assumption, these books are not historical in the correct sense of the word. They were not contemporary or contemporaneous accounts of events narrated in them, and were not written by the disciples of Jesus, their followers, or anyone who witnessed the events. The introduction to the gospels in the New Revised Standard Version of the Bible, affirms that the gospels whose aim was 'to confirm Christian faith', were written not earlier than forty to sixty years (presumably much later)[1] after the reported death of Jesus and 'do not present eyewitness or contemporary accounts of Jesus' life and teaching'.[2] 'The patient work of historical research,' has also shown that, 'the gospel accounts as we now have them were the consolidation of individual pieces of material, remembered and passed along through oral tradition for at least a generation or two before anything was put down in writing'.[3]

---

[1] These were the earliest possible speculative dates, with the real dates unknown. There are however indications that the earliest gospels were not written until late in the second century CE. See DM Murdock, *Who was Jesus: Fingerprints of the Christ* (Stellar House Publishing 2011) 59-83.

[2] *The Bible, New Revised Standard Version* (with Apocrypha) (Oxford University Press 2001) 1744.

[3] GF Chesnut, *Images of Christ: An Introduction to Christology* (Seabury Press 1984) 114-136.

Like most of the other books of the Bible, the gospels were the works of unknown persons.[4] It is only church tradition that ascribed their authorship to the persons whose names they bear with a view to lending them credence as authentic eyewitness accounts,[5] even though there is no evidence for this, and realistically, these people could not have written them.[6] Thus, the church credits the authorship of Matthew's gospel to the disciple Matthew, John's gospel to the 'beloved disciple', Mark's gospel to a companion of Peter, and Luke's gospel to a companion of Paul. It is also church tradition that ascribes authorship of Acts of the Apostles to Luke, the said companion of Paul.[7] These ascriptions of authorship and the accounts of the gospels are, however, unfounded.

---

[4] For a suggestion that the Flavian dynastic family of Rome invented Christianity and the gospels in order to remove Jewish militancy and transform the Jewish religion and the nature of their expected Messiah, see J Atwil, *Caesar's Messiah: The Roman Conspiracy to Invent Jesus* (CreateSpace 2011).

[5] This was the common practice at that time of pseudo-epigraphy. See the introductions to the gospels in the *New Oxford Annotated Bible,* supra n 17, ch. 2. See also BD Ehrman, *Whose word Is It? The Story behind who changed the New Testament and Why* (The Continuum International Publishing Group 2006. See also RL Fox, *The Unauthorised Version* (Penguin Books 1991), 114-136, 137-145.

[6] See the Introduction to the gospels of Matthew, Mark, Luke and John in the *New Oxford Annotated Bible, New Oxford Annotated Bible, NRSV with the Apocrypha* (4thed) (Oxford University Press 2010) 1746, 1791, 1827 and 1879. See also the *Catholic Encyclopaedia,* http://www.newadvent.org/cathen/10057a.htm; http://www.newadvent.org/cathen/09674b.htm#II; http://www.newadvent.org/cathen/09420a.htm; http://www.newadvent.org/cathen/01117a.htm. See further, Myth No. 4 in, D Fitzgerald, Fitzgerald D, *Nailed: Ten Myths that Show Jesus Never Existed at All* (Lulu.com 2010); DM Murdock, *Who was Jesus: Fingerprints of the Christ* (Stellar house Publishing 2011)1, 60-64.

[7] See the Introduction to Acts of the Apostles in the *New Oxford Annotated Bible, New Oxford Annotated Bible, NRSV with the Apocrypha* (4thed) (Oxford University Press 2010) 1919.

First, although tradition holds that Mark was a follower of Peter in the course of his preaching in Rome, the purported preaching of Peter in Rome and the followership of Mark rest only on church tradition.[8] There is no evidence in the Bible that Peter preached outside Israel. On the contrary, the Bible shows clearly that he and the other disciples concentrated any work they did in Israel and resisted preaching to or converting Gentiles.[9] If the tradition were correct that Luke, a companion of Paul, wrote the gospel bearing his name as well as Acts of the Apostles, it would mean that, like Paul, he wrote without being a follower of Jesus, or a witness to the events he purported to narrate. As for the authorship of Matthew and John's gospels by the disciples of Jesus bearing those names, it is noteworthy that these, as well as other books of the New Testament, were written originally in Greek from which they were translated into Latin and later English. Since the disciples of Jesus were illiterate villagers who only spoke their local dialect, Aramaic, they could not have written in Greek – the language of the educated or travelled.[10] Moreover, since neither Jesus nor his disciples left any records about themselves or their activities, these accounts could not have come from their memoirs. In spite of this and the long lapse of time between the alleged events and the story, the gospels, especially John's, make extensive verbatim quotations purporting to be from Jesus.

---

[8] See the *Catholic Encyclopaedia,*
http://www.newadvent.org/cathen/09674b.htm#II.
[9] See e.g., Matthew 10:5-7; 15:21-28; Mark 7:24-30; Matthew 19:22-29; Galatians 2:7-9.
[10] See e.g., Acts 4:13.

Second, the stories about Jesus do not give objective accounts of events, their purposes being unabashedly to affirm and consolidate belief in him and promote evangelization.[11] In the introduction to Luke's gospel, the author acknowledging that he was not an eyewitness to the events therein narrated. Instead, he states that having undertaken a careful investigation of the issues, he 'decided to write an orderly account [...] so that you may know the certainty of the things you have been taught'. The same writer continued his hearsay and hortatory narrative about Jesus in Acts of the Apostles.[12] It is also beyond doubt that the gospels have undergone many alterations, interpolations, and changes in the course of their copying and transmission; that many different manuscripts of the same gospels exist; that the current gospels are not original; and that the earliest gospels in use did not appear until centuries after the events they report.[13] Interestingly, the Epistles of Paul written before any of the gospels for the affirmation of Jesus as Christ and instruction of believers, did not attempt to give any historical narratives of the life and ministry of Jesus and did not make any quotations of his statements or teachings.

---

[11] See John 20:31; EP Sanders, *The Historical Figure of Jesus* (London: Penguin Books 1995) 3-4.

[12] See Acts 1:1-11.

[13] For a comprehensive discussion of this, see BD Ehrman, *Whose Word Is It? The Story behind who changed the New Testament and Why* (The Continuum International Publishing Group 2006). See also, RL Fox, *The Unauthorised Version* (Penguin Books 1991) 114-136.

Different Gospels for Different Believers

It is instructive that originally Christians had no unity in their choice or use of gospels. While some Christians used only Matthew, those who did not believe that Jesus was the Christ used only Mark. Others like Marcion and his followers accepted only parts of Luke, while Gnostic Christians who did not believe in a human Jesus accepted only John.[14] Eventually, it was resolved on the insistence of Bishop Irenaeus of Lyon in about 180 CE, that all Christians should use the four gospels. According to him, there are four zones and four winds in the world to which the gospel had spread; and since the gospels are the pillars of the church, it is fitting to have four gospels to represent the four zones and winds.[15]

In addition to the four canonical gospels, there are numerous other gospels telling divergent stories about Jesus. These include the Gospel of Peter and the Infancy Gospel of Thomas. They also include the Gospels of Judas, Mary, James, Hebrews and Egyptians. Apart from the above, there were many other Christian writings, including acts and epistles, circulating in the decades and centuries following the emergence of Christianity. Out of these numerous sources, only twenty-seven eventually made it into the New Testament. The first time these books became canon was in 367 CE when Bishop Athanasius of Alexandria wrote to the churches under his diocese

---

[14] For a discussion of this and other questions concerning the New Testament, see BD Ehrman, supra n 13, 34-35. See also, Myth No. 8, in D Fitzgerald, *Nailed: Ten Myths that Show Jesus Never Existed at All* (Lulu.com 2010).

[15] Ibid, 35. See also *The Catholic Encyclopaedia,* http://www.newadvent.org/cathen/03274a.htm.

advising them to that effect. This canonisation would ultimately, and after long squabbles, be accepted by the church hierarchy as the New Testament. The books that failed to make the list were termed non-canonical.[16] Thus, far from being the product of divine inspiration and mandate, the contents of the New Testament as we know it today, were decided by church leaders.

Given the above analysis and the inconsistencies, contradictions and fabrications we saw in previous chapters, the Bible has not provided any reliable account of the life and times of Jesus Christ. As has also been noted, in spite of claims in the New Testament to the contrary, neither the Old Testament, nor the prophecies contained therein, back up the story of Jesus. Unless the New Testament narratives about Jesus find significant corroboration in secular history, they must be taken in the same way as the narratives of the scriptures of sundry religions – as matters of faith rather than fact.

What does History say about Jesus Christ?

The question as to what history records about Jesus Christ has been the subject of much inquiry.[17] Incidentally, history does not offer any help on the person of Jesus or his story as recorded in the Bible. There is practically no contemporaneous or contemporary historical record of the person, life, ministry, teachings, death, resurrection and

---

[16] See BD Ehrman, supra n 13, 35-36.
[17] See A Schweitzer, *The Quest of the Historical Jesus* (New York: Dover Publications Inc. 2005) for a comprehensive examination and analysis of the various studies on the historicity of Jesus Christ. See also GA Wells, *The Jesus Legend* (Chicago: Open Quest 1996).

ascension of Jesus. As observed by the Oxford Dictionary of the Bible, 'outside the NT (New Testament of the Bible), there is little recorded about "Jesus of Nazareth."'[18] The Catholic Encyclopaedia and other apologetic writings on the 'historical' Jesus also confirm that the only significant source of information about him is the Bible, notably the gospels, the Acts of the Apostles and the Epistles of Paul.[19] Philo Judaeus,[20] (Philo of Alexandria) a prominent Jewish historian who lived at about the same time Jesus supposedly lived and during the early decades of Christianity, exhibited no knowledge of Jesus Christ and Christians in his writings despite the prominence of that city in early Christianity.[21] Despite these definite and unambiguous affirmations that information about Jesus come only from the Bible and that secular history has no significant record of him or his activities, strenuous attempts have been made by apologists to show that history proves the story of Jesus.

The chief historical work often relied on to 'prove' the historicity of Jesus is Flavius Josephus's book, *the Antiquities of the Jews.* The relevant passage, the so-called *Testimonium Flavianum,* is contained in Book 18, Chapter 3, and Paragraph 3. Josephus was not a contemporary of Jesus or a witness to the events in his life, having been born in 37 CE. However, he had lived in Cana, and was at a time

---

[18] WRF Browning, *Oxford Dictionary of the Bible* (Oxford University Press 2009) 171.
[19] See the *Catholic Encyclopaedia*, http://www.newadvent.org/cathen/08375a.htm. See also EP Sanders, supra n 11, 3-4.
[20] He was born between 15-10 BCE and died between 45-50 CE.
[21] See K Humphries, http://www.jesusneverexisted.com/philo.html.

the governor of Galilee – the area in which the gospels located many of Jesus' activities. Since Josephus lived in the 1st Century CE in the same area where Jesus and his disciples supposedly lived and ministered, he should know some things about Jesus Christ. However, Josephus' only apparent reference to Jesus was in this singular paragraph:

> *Now, there was about this time, Jesus, a wise man, if it be lawful to call him a man, for he was a doer of wonderful works, a teacher of such men as receive the truth with pleasure. He drew over to him both many of the Jews, and many of the Gentiles. He was the Christ; and when Pilate, at the suggestion of the principal men amongst us, had condemned him to the cross, those that loved him at the first did not forsake him, for he appeared to them alive again the third day, as the divine prophets had foretold these and ten thousand other wonderful things concerning him; and the tribe of Christians, so named from him, are not extinct at this day.*

This reference in *The Antiquities of the Jews* is widely acknowledged to have been a forgery wholly or partially added to the original writing by the Church more than 400 years after the time of Jesus.[22] Before that time, no one – even those who knew all about the book – had seen that paragraph.[23] In particular, one of the most prominent church fathers, Origen, while defending the historicity of Jesus, had quoted

---

[22] See *The Catholic Encyclopaedia,*
http://www.newadvent.org/cathen/08522a.htm; WRF Browning (ed.) supra n 18, 177; IM Zeitlin, *Jesus and the Judaism of His Time* (Policy Press 1988) 139-140.
[23] The Church Fathers, notably Justin Martyr, Iranaeus (of France), Clement (of Alexandria), Tertulian (of Carthage), Cyprian (of Carthage) and Arnobius (of Sicca) and Origen (of Alexandria) all of whom had written extensively in defence of the historicity of Jesus made no reference to this seemingly very important passage.

extensively from the book, without referring to the *Testimonium Flavianum*, the paragraph that would most have helped his cause had it been in existence. He also expressly stated that Josephus did not believe that Jesus was the Christ. Moreover, the paragraph was not in the earlier versions of the book, including the version written in the 3rd Century AD.[24]

That the *Testimonium Flavianum* must have been a forgery rather than a true historical account is evident from the way it lumps together in one short paragraph and without any detail or elaboration, all the essential claims about Jesus in the gospels.[25] Besides, the tone of the statement, which appears out of context, was neither factual, objective, nor detached. Chapter 3 of book 18 discussed the Jewish rebellion against some of Pilate's policies and the attempts to subjugate them under Roman control. In the middle of that discourse, the *Testimonium Flavianum* suddenly appears. Immediately after that, the next paragraph continues the discussion of the misfortune of the Jews. Since the Jews were the ones who reportedly clamoured for Jesus to be crucified and ostensibly forced Pilate's hand on that, it is difficult to see how the story of Jesus could fit into a discussion of Jewish misfortunes in the hands of Rome and Pilate. It is clear, therefore, that the passage in *The Antiquities of the Jews*, does not provide any historical evidence of Jesus or the stories about him.[26]

---

[24] See K Humphreys, *Jesus Never Existed,*
http://www.jesusneverexisted.com/josephus-etal.html.
[25] WRF Browning, supra n 18, 177.
[26] See EP Sanders, supra n 11, 50-51.

In addition, Josephus had in another book, *The War of the Jews*,[27] written in some detail about many self-proclaimed Jewish messiahs without mentioning Jesus of Nazareth. These included Judas of Galilee, Theudas the Magician, and the 'Egyptian Jew'. Others were, Jesus ben Pandira (a miracle worker and end-time preacher who was crucified on the eve of Passover during the reign of Alexander Jannaeus, King of Judea who ruled from 103 to 76 BC), Jesus ben Ananias (a doomsday prophet), and Jesus ben Saphat (an insurrectionist against the Roman authorities).[28] It is probable that the story of one or some of these prophets and agitators, especially Jesus ben Pandira, inspired the legend of the gospel Jesus.[29] In the context of these pseudo-messiahs and as an Orthodox Jew, Josephus could not have believed that Jesus was the messiah whom the Jews awaited – a point made by Origen above. Accordingly, there would be no reason or basis for him to affirm that Jesus 'was the Christ'.

Another historical source often cited on the historicity of Jesus Christ is Tacitus. According to the Catholic Encyclopaedia, Tacitus[30] recorded that Pontius Pilate executed the founder of Christianity, which he described as a deadly superstition, under the reign of Emperor Tiberius. He also recorded that Christianity withstood suppression by the Romans; that Emperor Nero wrongly accused them

---

[27] F Josephus, *The Wars of the Jews* (Palatine Press 2015).
[28] Ibid.
[29] See G Massey, *The Historical Jesus and the Mythical Christ* (Forgotten Books) 1-4; www.forgottenbooks.org; Gerald Massey, *Gerald Massey's Lectures* (California: The Book Tree 2008) 1-4.
[30] Publius (Gaius) Cornelius Tacitus.

of starting the fire in Rome; and that the Romans regarded Christianity as a sect of Jewish religion.[31] Nevertheless, Tacitus only confirmed the existence of Christians, but said nothing about the life and ministry of Jesus. As a Roman writer who lived between 55 and 120 CE, well after the year of Jesus' supposed death, he was in no position to provide, and did not provide, any corroboration of the events narrated in the gospels.

Gaius Suetonius,[32] who lived between 69 and 135 CE, was another Roman historian that gets a mention. He apparently regarded Jesus Christ as 'a Roman insurgent who stirred up seditions under the reign of Claudius (41-54 CE)' and reported that Emperor Nero treated Christians 'severely'.[33] Again, this Roman writer said nothing about the life of Jesus, his ministry or any of the events associated with him; and the insurgent he referred to only lived about half a century after the time of Jesus. In any event, this historian was born more than sixty years after the time of Jesus and was very far from Palestine where his ministry supposedly took place.

The last historian usually cited in connection with the historical Jesus Christ is Pliny the Younger,[34] a Roman Governor of Bithynia, who lived between 61 and 112 CE. His supposed contribution to the historicity of Jesus was a letter he sent to the Roman Emperor Trajan

---

[31] See *The Catholic Encyclopaedia*,
http://www.newadvent.org/cathen/08375a.htm.
[32] Gaius Seutonius Tranquillus.
[33] See *The Catholic Encyclopaedia*,
http://www.newadvent.org/cathen/08375a.htm.
[34] Gaius Plinius Caecillius Secundus.

on how to deal with Christians in his jurisdiction and their 'extravagant and perverse superstition' in their allegiance to Christ 'whom they celebrated as their God'.[35] This letter, however, is only a *post-facto* affirmation of the existence of Christians and does not affirm the stories about Jesus Christ or the doctrines underpinning the Christian faith. Interestingly, Pliny the Elder,[36] the uncle of Pliny the Younger, and a renowned historian who helped in training and educating him, did not say anything about Jesus in his own works even though he lived nearer the time of Jesus. Clearly, therefore, none of these historians or indeed any other contemporary or near contemporary historian said anything significant about the person, life or ministry of Jesus, or confirmed any of the events in the gospels. Instead, the most credit they gave to the Christ story is the existence or activities of Christians, a matter that was never in dispute.[37]

'Historical' Reconstructions of Jesus Christ

Although history is silent about Jesus of Nazareth, apologetic historians and theologians have for centuries tried to squeeze water out of stone in attempts to discover the 'historical Jesus'. However, after reviewing the efforts of numerous historians in the 18th and 19th Century in this regard, the renowned Christian theologian, Albert

---

[35] See *The Catholic Encyclopaedia,* http://www.newadvent.org/cathen/08375a.htm.

[36] Gaius Pliny Secundus (AD 23 – 79).

[37] See DM Murdock, *Who was Jesus: Fingerprints of the Christ* (Stellar house Publishing 2011) 86 – 98.

Schweitzer concludes that the Jesus of the gospels was entirely eschatological and did not exist in history:

> *There is nothing more negative than the result of the critical study of the life of Jesus. The Jesus of Nazareth, who preached the ethic of the Kingdom of God, who founded the Kingdom of Heaven upon earth and died to give His work its final consecration, never had any existence. He is a figure designed by rationalism, endowed with life by liberalism, and clothed by modern theology in an historical garb.*[38]

Consistent with the above conclusion, many prominent historians – Christian and Secular – have over the past centuries questioned the historicity of gospel narratives of Jesus and regarded them as essentially dogmatic, mythical or lacking of reliable proof.[39] This notwithstanding, modern Christologists have striven to make a case for the historical Jesus. However, their 'histories' or 'lives' of Jesus have in effect been attempts historically to re-construct Jesus based on information contained in the gospels, and the authors' faith and points of view.[40] As Stephen Evans has observed:

---

[38] A Schweitzer, supra n 17, 396. This work is so extensive on the subject, that no useful purpose would be served here by going through the different attempts by different authors to identify the 'historical' Jesus.

[39] For a discussion of this, see GF Chesnut, supra n 3; GA Wells, supra n 17.

[40] See e.g., E Renan, *The Life of Jesus* (New York: Random house 1972; HE Forsdick, *The Man from Nazareth* (New York: Harper & Brothers 1949) 244; JD Crossan, *The Historical Jesus: The Life of a Mediterranean Jewish Peasant* (San Francisco: Harper 1991). See also JP Mackey, *Jesus the Man and the Myth* (SCM Press Ltd 1979); AN Wilson, *Jesus* (London: Sinclair Stevenson 1992); B Thiering, *Jesus the Man: A New Interpretation from the Dead Sea Scrolls* (London: Doubleday 1992). See further, V Kuster, *The Many Faces of Jesus Christ* (Neukirchener Verlag 1999; translated by John Bowden 2001); G Stanton, *The Gospels and Jesus* (Second ed) (Oxford university Press 2002); J Crossley, *Jesus and the Chaos of History: Redirecting the Life of the Historical Jesus* (Oxford

> *Whether supported by fancy historical methodology or not, truncated lives of Jesus still seem to tell more about the authors than about the historical Jesus. Liberation theologians give us Jesus as political revolutionary, feminists see Jesus as proto-feminist, and various academic portraits show us a Jesus who is politically correct [...] This point is by now a commonplace insight, but that has not dissuaded scholars and non-scholars from continuing to produce personal versions of the 'real' historical Jesus.*[41]

The quest for the historical Jesus therefore, has been likened to the case of a man, 'who peers into a deep well but sees only his own face staring back at him'.[42] If we were even to discover the real historical Jesus, Schweitzer ventures to submit that, 'He will not be a Jesus Christ to whom the religion of the present can ascribe, according to its long-cherished custom, its own thoughts and ideas, as it did with the Jesus of its own making'.[43]

The question then arises as to why history would be so silent about Jesus Christ if he did live. According to the Catholic Encyclopaedia,[44] the dearth of information about Jesus from non-Christian sources was due to the fact that both Jews and pagans viewed Christians with hatred and contempt and did not expect that Christianity would go on to become an important religion. It also explains that historical

---

University Press 2015); GSJ O' Collins, *Christology: A Biblical, historical and Systematic Study of Jesus* (Oxford University Press 1995).

[41] CS Evans, *The Historical Christ and the Jesus of Faith: The Incarnational Theory as History* (Oxford: Clarendon Press 1996) 40.

[42] G Tyrell, *Christianity at the Crossroads* (London: Longmans, Green & Co., 1909), 44. Quoted in CS Evans, *The Historical Christ and the Jesus of Faith: the Incarnational Theory as History* (Oxford: Clarendon Press, 1996) 39.

[43] A Schweitzer, supra n 3, 398-399.

[44] http://www.newadvent.org/cathen/08375a.htm.

recordings were not very common during the time of Jesus; and that Judea was a relatively obscure and insignificant place within the Roman Empire. These explanations however, lack merit.

The claim that Jews and Gentiles alike did not expect the ministry of Jesus to be great contradicts reports in the gospels about the miraculous circumstances of Jesus' conception and birth, the huge followership he drew in the course of his ministry[45] and the numerous miracles he performed. It contradicts reports in the gospels that Jesus was famous throughout Israel and nearby nations[46] and the record of amazing and hitherto unseen events attending his death, such as an earthquake, total eclipse of the sun and mass resurrection of dead saints.[47] It also contradicts the claim that Jesus resurrected from the dead and ascended into heaven in the sight of people.[48] In short, many of the events narrated by the gospels as surrounding Jesus are so unusual and so astounding that historians could not have ignored them. Historians record significant events as they unfold or shortly thereafter on their own merit, rather than in anticipation of the future greatness or otherwise of the characters involved.

Moreover, the fact that people do not approve of a particular person does not mean that historians of the day would ignore them altogether. Although they might give events in the life of that person different interpretations or colorations depending on their prejudices, they

---

[45] See Mark 5:24; Matthew 8:1; John 6:2.
[46] See Mark 1:28; Luke 4:14; Matthew 4:24.
[47] See Chapter 8.
[48] See Chapters 9 and 10.

would still record them – somehow. Indeed, and as earlier noted, Jewish history records the ministry of many people, including some named Jesus, who had dubiously claimed to be the Messiah or God although most of their contemporaries must have regarded them with incredulity, lack of seriousness or outright contempt.[49]

Furthermore, the explanations assume that everybody in Israel hated Jesus and Christians, when this could not have been true, according to the Bible. Certainly, the multitudes of followers and admirers of Jesus, including his disciples, several women, and beneficiaries of his miracles, could not have hated him. Similarly, the Roman soldiers, who were convinced of the innocence and divinity of Jesus, could not have hated him. Even Pontius Pilate could not have hated him, going by the gospel story. Why did none of these people or their sympathisers record any of the events in the gospels? Most importantly perhaps, why did the disciples not record anything about Jesus when they were supposedly his closest contemporaries and eyewitnesses to his activities, especially when all of them, except Judas Iscariot, outlived him?

Finally, the claim is not correct that there was a dearth of historical records at the time of Jesus, or that Judea was an insignificant part of the Roman Empire. On the converse, that period and the decades immediately following it were arguably the most recorded in ancient

---

[49] For an account of these, see *The Jewish Encyclopaedia,* http://www.jewishencyclopedia.com/articles/12416-pseudo-messiahs. See Chapters 13 and 14.

history, being the classical period when the Roman Empire was near its greatest. At that time, Judea was an essential, and oftentimes, rebellious part of the Empire, with the Jewish revolts of 66 - 70 CE being among the most serious ever faced by the Roman authorities. As observed by David Fitzgerald:

> *The first century is actually considered one of the best documented periods in ancient history and Judea, far from being a forgotten backwater, was a turbulent province of vital strategic importance to the Romans. There were plenty of writers, both Roman and Jewish, who had great interest in and much to say about the region and its happenings during Jesus' time.*[50]

The First Century CE also corresponds with the period when, according to the New Testament and Christian tradition, early Christians faced numerous prosecutions; thus, the more reason why events surrounding Jesus and his ministry, should have been historically attested. Certainly, the trial and execution of Jesus by Pontius Pilate, as well as the execution of Steven by Jewish authorities for blasphemy, would have been recorded in Roman and Jewish annals if they had in fact happened.

It would seem therefore, that the belief in Jesus and his work of salvation rest, not on facts, but on popular myths and religious philosophy similar to those of some other ancient religions. In spite of

---

[50] See Myth No. 2 in, D Fitzgerald, *Nailed: Ten Myths that Show Jesus Never Existed at All* (Lulu.com 2010).

this, Christian churches have for over two millennia continued to broadcast the story of Jesus' divinity and the salvation he supposedly wrought for humanity to both believers and non-believers.

CHAPTER 13

WAS JESUS DIVINE?

In the beginning was the Word, and the Word was with God, and the Word was God. He was in the beginning with God. All things were made through him, and without him nothing was made that was made. In him was life, and the life was the light of men. - John 1:1- 4 (NKJV)

The preceding chapters have established the dubiousness and incredibility of the story of the life, ministry, passion, resurrection and ascension of ascension. That should be enough to end this book. However, it is necessary to consider whether Jesus Christ, *assuming that he did live*, could have been divine as the Bible's New Testament claims. In addition to the extraordinary tales concerning his conception, birth and infancy, statements as to the divinity and prior heavenly existence of Jesus occur in a number of passages in the Bible. The Christian belief, as earlier stated, is that Jesus, as God, took the form of a man and came to the world to die in order to accomplish the divine purpose of human salvation. At other times, the New Testament describes Jesus in exclusive messianic terms as the *Son of God*, or the *Son of Man*. Could Jesus really have been God or the Son of God?

Was Jesus God?[1]

The gospel of John declares that, Jesus as 'the Word' existed with God from the beginning; was instrumental to the creation of all things; and was the source of life for humanity.[2] Jesus reportedly affirmed this claim[3] and added that he was in existence before the birth of Abraham.[4] In apparent exercise of divine prerogative, Jesus forgave sins[5] and received worship.[6] Further, Jesus told his disciples that anyone who had seen him had seen God the father[7] and pointedly declared that he 'and the Father are one'.[8] Although, at the soul level, all humans are one with God, Jesus undoubtedly implied that he was materially the very expression of God, an expression that does not include other human beings. This interpretation is consistent with other claims in the New Testament that Jesus was God. In Philippians 2:5-11, Paul admonishes believers to let their attitude be the same as that of Jesus:

> *Who, being in very nature God, did not consider equality with God something to be grasped, but made himself nothing, taking the very nature of a servant, being made in human likeness. And being found in appearance as a man, he humbled himself and became obedient to death – even death on a cross!*[9]

---

[1] The word "God" in this section is used synonymously with YHWH, the Jewish Deity.

[2] John 1:1-4.

[3] See John 17:5

[4] See John 8:58.

[5] See e.g., Luke 7:48; Mark 2:1-2; Luke 5:20, 24; 7:48.

[6] See e.g., Matthew 2:2, 8, 11; 14:3; 28:9, 17; John 9:38.

[7] John 14:9.

[8] John 10:30. See also John 1:18.

[9] Emphasis added.

Similarly, in Colossians, Paul asserts that Jesus was the image of the invisible God, and the firstborn of all creation, through whom all things in heaven and earth came into being.[10] He also asserts that, *in Christ all the fullness of the Deity lives in bodily form'.*[11] In 1 Corinthians 10:4, 10, Paul identifies Jesus with Yahweh who had assisted and punished the Israelites during their time in the wilderness following their exodus from Egypt. Rationalising the incarnation of God as Jesus, Apostle Paul states:

> *Since the children have flesh and blood, he too shared in their humanity so that by his death he might break the power of him who holds the power of death - that is, the devil - and free those who all their lives were held in slavery by their fear of death. For surely it is not angels he helps, but Abraham's descendants. For this, reason he had to be made like them, fully human in every way, in order that he might become a merciful and faithful high priest in service to God, and that he might make atonement for the sins of the people. Because he himself suffered when he was tempted, he is able to help those who are being tempted.*[12]

Apart from his description as God, the New Testament describes Jesus as the Son of God, even before his conception.[13] According to John's gospel, Jesus is 'the only begotten Son of God', who due to his love of the world, God sent for the salvation of all who believe in him.[14] Numerous other passages in the New Testament also describe Jesus

---

[10] See Colossians 1:15-18. See also 1 Corinthians 8:6.
[11] Colossians 2:9, emphasis added.
[12] Hebrews 2:14-18.
[13] See Luke 1:35.
[14] See John 3:16.

as the Son of God.[15] In addition, Jesus was called 'the Son of Man',[16] a phrase he repeatedly applied to himself[17] and which though suggesting humanity[18] connotes messiahship. One could however, repudiate the supposed deity or divinity of Jesus on several grounds.

First, as noted in Chapter 2, Jesus was supposed to be a descendant of King David and the inheritor of the Davidic dynasty in accordance with Jewish messianic prophecies. For this purpose, his blood lineage was traced to David and ultimately to Adam. Pursuant to these claims, the Bible teaches that Jesus was fully human, although he was also fully God. However, as was discussed in that chapter, if Jesus was truly a man who descended biologically from the lineage of David, he would not be God and would not have come down from heaven. Conversely, if he was truly God, he could not have descended from David.

Second, the supposed deity of a Jewish Jesus is inconsistent with Jewish henotheism. For the Jews, although there are other Gods, only Yahweh is theirs, and he would not share his divinity with anyone else. In Deuteronomy 4:35, Yahweh pointedly tells the Israelites:

> *I am the LORD, and there is none else, there is no God beside me: I girded thee, though thou hast not known me. That they*

---

[15] See, e.g. Matthew 14:33; 27:54; Mark 15:39; Luke 3:38; John 1:18; 5:18-23; 20:31; 1 john 4:9; 5:9-12; Romans 1:4; Hebrews 1:2; 5; Galatians 4:4.
[16] See Mark 3:38; Luke 5:24; John 3:13; 6:62; Acts 7:56; Revelation 1:13.

[17] See e.g., Mark 10:45; Matthew 8:20; 12:32, 26:63-64; Luke 9:58; John 9:35.
[18] See e.g., Daniel 7:13-14; Psalm 8:4; Numbers 23:19.

*may know from the rising of the sun, and from the west, that
there is none beside me. I am the LORD, and there is none
else.*[19]

Accordingly, the first of the Ten Commandments decrees that the
Israelites must not have any other God except Yahweh who brought
them out of Egypt.[20] Isaiah 42:8 and 48:11 further make it clear that
Yahweh will neither yield his glory nor share it with any person. The
belief in the exclusivity of the deity of Yahweh is encapsulated in
arguably the most important Jewish prayer, *The Shema*, as follows:
*'Hear, O Israel: The Lord our God, the Lord is one. Love the Lord
your God with all your heart and with all your soul and with all your
mind and with all your strength.'*[21] In short, once the Israelites
officially adopted him as their God, the expression of the belief in the
exclusive deity of Yahweh in the Hebrew Scriptures became absolute
and pervasive.[22] For the Jews therefore, the notion of Jesus of
Nazareth as God would be anathema.[23]

Third, despite suggestions to the contrary in John's gospel and the
Epistles of Paul as seen above, Jesus himself apparently affirmed the

---

[19] See also Isaiah 45:5-6.

[20] Deuteronomy 5:6-10 and Exodus 20:2-3.

[21] Deuteronomy 6:5-9.

[22] The exclusivity of the divinity of Yahweh in the Bible is notorious. See e.g.,
Deuteronomy 6:4; 39: 39; 2 Samuel 7:22; 22:32; I kings 8:60; 2 kings 19:15;
1Chronicles 17:20; Psalm 18:31; 86:10; Isaiah 44:8; Nehemiah 9:6; Joel 2:27.

[23] It must be observed that ancient Israelites were also polytheists for long periods
of their biblical history, until the onset of the Mosaic Legal system. Despite this
however, they continued to worship many of the deities worshipped by
neighbouring nations, leading on numerous occasions to the apparent wrath and
punishment of Yahweh.

exclusive deity of Yahweh and showed in many places that he did not see himself as God. In Mark 12:29-30, he re-stated to the approval of his listeners, *The Shema*. In John 17:3, he stated that, 'now this is eternal life: that they know you, the only true God, and Jesus Christ, whom you have sent'. Being 'sent' by God is not indicative of divinity since according to the Bible, God had sent to the Israelites all the prophets of the Old Testament. Further, on many occasions, Jesus prayed to God or indicated that he was merely an agent for the doing of God's will. [24] In John 17:4-6, for example, he prayed to God:

> *I have brought you glory on earth by finishing the work you gave me to do. And now, Father, glorify me in your presence with the glory I had with you before the world began. "I have revealed you to those whom you gave me out of the world. They were yours; you gave them to me and they have obeyed your word.*

Other passages in the New Testament also affirm that there is only one God. According to 1 Timothy 2:5, 'there is one God and one mediator between God and mankind, the man Christ Jesus.'[25] A mediator between God and human beings cannot be the God. Thus, Galatians 3:20 states that, 'a mediator, however, implies more than one party; but God is one'. 1 Corinthians 8:4-6 expresses the point clearly:

> *There is no God but one. For even if there are so-called gods, whether in heaven or on earth (as indeed there are many 'gods' and many 'Lords'), yet for us there is but one God, the Father, from whom all things came and for whom we live; and*

---

[24] See, e.g., Mark 1:35; Matthew 11:25-26; 14:23; Luke 6:12; 22:41-44; John 11:41-42; 12:27-28; Hebrews 5:7.
[25] See further Hebrews 8:6; 9:15; 12:24.

there is but one Lord, Jesus Christ, through whom all things came and through whom we live.[26]

Indeed, the notion that Jesus was God, and the doctrine of Holy Trinity, are reflective of rampant 'pagan' polytheism and the polytheism of the Jews before their adoption of Yahweh as exclusive deity.[27]

Fourth, and helped by the conflicting messages given by the Bible, there existed much disagreement and disputation among different sects of Christianity on the nature of Jesus.[28] Many, such as the Ebionites, believed that he was entirely human, a belief consistent with the synoptic gospels' indication that Jesus gained divinity after his baptism when he was 'adopted' by God – an adoption that was subsequently confirmed during his transfiguration.[29] Consistent with the stance of John's gospel and Apostle Paul, many on the other hand, including the Gnostics and Marcion of Sinope and his followers, did not believe that Jesus was human at all, but that he only appeared to be human when he was in fact always spiritual and divine.[30] Therefore, the Epistle of John complains that, 'many deceivers, who do not acknowledge Jesus Christ as coming in the flesh, have gone out

---

[26] See also James 2:19; Ephesians 4:6; 1 Timothy 1:17.

[27] See J Hastings (ed.) *Encyclopaedia of Religion and Ethics* (Edinburgh: T and T Clark 1971) 408.

[28] For some discussion of the controversy, see GF Chesnut, *Images of Christ: An Introduction to Christology* (Seabury Press 1984) 93-105.

[29] See Mark 1:9-11; Luke 3:21; Matthew 17:1-13; Luke 9:28-36; Mark 9:2-13. See also the *Catholic Encyclopaedia,* http://www.newadvent.org/cathen/01150a.htm.

[30] This doctrine is known as Docetism and was championed by Marcion and Gnostic Christians. Bishop Ignatius of Antioch declared it a heresy in the year 107.

into the world', and denounces such people as 'the deceiver and the antichrist',[31] and 'wicked'.[32]

It was not until the Council of Nicea in 325 AD that the church agreed on the doctrine of the divinity of a human Jesus.[33] At that council, Emperor Constantine proposed a solution acceptable to the delegates that Jesus Christ was of 'the same substance' as the Father. The Nicene Creed, which was the product of that convention, states in part that Christians believe:

> *in one Lord Jesus Christ, the only begotten Son of God, and born of the Father before all ages. God of God, light of light, true God of true God. Begotten not made, consubstantial to the Father, by whom all things were made. Who for us men and for our salvation came down from heaven.* And was *incarnate of the Holy Ghost and of the Virgin Mary and was made man.*[34]

Subsequent to the Council of Nicea, and in spite of this Creed, many prominent Christians, including bishops, continued to teach that Jesus was only divine and not truly human; and that his divinity subsumed his humanity.[35] This position, which the church in fact confirmed at the Second Council of Ephesus in 449 AD,[36] led to further serious schisms in early Christendom. Eventually, the Council of Chalcedon

---

[31] 2 John 1:7.

[32] 2 John 1:11.

[33] The Roman Emperor Constantine convened the Council (a synod of all bishops of the church) on 19 June 325.

[34] See *The Catholic Encyclopaedia*, http://www.newadvent.org/cathen/11049a.htm, emphasis added.

[35] This is the so-called Monophysite doctrine.

[36] Designated the 'Robber Synod' by Pope Leo 1.

of 451 AD resolved this further controversy.[37] In line with the Tome of Pope Leo 1, the Council issued a statement that Jesus had a dual nature – fully divine and fully human, though without sin – and that both natures exist without confusion, contradiction or change.[38] According to the Catholic Encyclopaedia, the doctrine of divine incarnation implies, 'the Divine Person of Jesus Christ; the Human Nature of Jesus Christ; the Hypostatic Union of the Human with the Divine Nature in the Divine Person of Jesus Christ.'[39]

Fifth, the designation as the 'Son of God' was not exclusive to Jesus. The Bible describes Yahweh as one of the sons of El,[40] and the kings of Israel as sons of God.[41] The people of Israel were also collectively designated the son of God.[42] If Jesus were the son of God because he was a descendant of Adam,[43] it would follow, by the Bible's own reckoning, that every human being is also a son or daughter of God since we are all supposed to have descended from Adam. In addition, although Colossians 1:15 refers to Jesus as the firstborn of all creation, Exodus 4:22, had already described Israel as the firstborn son of God. The New Testament also describes believers in Jesus Christ as sons

---

[37] Also known as the Fourth Ecumenical Council, the Council took place between 8 October to 1 November 451.
[38] See *The Catholic Encyclopaedia*,
http://www.newadvent.org/cathen/03555a.htm; see also *Encyclopaedia Britannica*,
https://www.britannica.com/topic/Incarnation-Jesus-Christ; D MacCulloch, *A History of Christianity* (Penguin Books 2012) 189-222.
[39] See *The Catholic Encyclopaedia*,
http://www.newadvent.org/cathen/07706b.htm.
[40] See e.g., Psalm 82; 89:5-6.
[41] See e.g., Psalm 2:7.
[42] See e.g. Hosea 11:1.
[43] However, it is evident from Chapter 2 that he was not.

and daughters of God.[44] Outside the Bible, Romans regarded Emperor Augustus as a son of God following the deification of his adoptive father, Emperor Julius Caesar.[45] The sons of other deified Roman Emperors and Egyptian Pharaohs were also 'sons of God'. In fact, the designation of national heroes as sons or daughters of God was common among different ancient cultures.[46]

Although the title 'the Son of God' as was used of Jesus Christ, suggests that he was the only heavenly son of God, the Bible says that sons of God of this type were many. In Genesis, sons of God reportedly came down from heaven to have sex with mortal women and thereby produce a race of giants.[47] Job 38:7, Psalm 82, and 89:6 all allude to the existence of many sons of God in heaven, while in the book of Daniel a heavenly being in the form of the Son of God appeared to be with Daniel in the fiery furnace.[48] In other religious mythologies, there were also many heavenly sons of God. In Greco-Roman mythology, Zeus or Jupiter – the king of the gods – begot many sons by having sexual relations with many gods and women. Aphrodite or Venus, the goddess of beauty and love, also had many lovers among gods and men and these were sons of God. Indeed, the

---

[44] 1 John 3:1; Galatians 3:26

[45] See WRF Browning (ed.) *Oxford Dictionary of the Bible* (Oxford University 2009) 337

[46] See e.g., R Warner, *Encyclopaedia of World Mythology* (BPC Publishing Limited London 1975) 25-28; P Wilkinson and N Phillip, *Mythology* (Doring Kindersley Ltd, London 2007); R Cavendish (ed.), *Legends of the World* (Orbis Publishing Ltd 1982); A Cotterell, *The Illustrated Encyclopaedia of Myths and Legends* (Marshall editions Ltd 1989).

[47] Genesis 6:1-4.

[48] See Daniel 3:25.

idea of gods copulating with humans and producing divine offspring was common in ancient mythologies.[49]

Sixth, Jesus is not the only person in the Bible described as 'the son of man'. The Old Testament uses the description in relation to Prophet Ezekiel,[50] the people of Israel,[51] and humanity in general.[52] Thus, the phrase suggests normal human beings rather than transcendental, super-human or divine ones. The dream in Daniel Chapter 7 regarding the 'son of man' was not about Jesus, as its interpretation in verses 15-28, makes it clear that it referred to anticipated political travails of the people of Israel and their liberation from the same in due course.

It is clear then, that the deity of a human Jesus as a foundational Christian doctrine, far from being universally accepted, was the eventual orthodox position adopted by the church among competing doctrines and forced down the throat of all believers.[53] However, many non-Trinitarian Christian denominations, to this day, do not accept this position.[54] As explained by the Church of the Great God,

> *The Trinity doctrine cannot be found in the Bible, as it was patched together by Catholic theologians hundreds of years after the deaths of the apostles and the completion of*

---

[49] See generally, A Cotterell, supra n 46.

[50] See the book of Ezekiel, from chapter 2.

[51] Daniel 13.

[52] See Psalm 8.

[53] See Myth No. 9 in D Fitzgerald, *Nailed: Ten Myths that Show Jesus Never Existed at All* (Lulu.com 2010).

[54] These include the Church of Jesus Christ of Latter Day Saints (Mormons), Jehovah's Witnesses; Church of the Great God; Christian Scientists, United Church of God, Unitarian Universalist Christians, Israelite Church of God in Jesus Christ, and Assemblies of Yahweh.

Scripture. Instead, Trinitarianism is a mixture of Jewish, Greek, and Roman philosophies, loosely based on a handful of Bible verses snatched out of context or interpolated into the text.[55]

Divinity of Kings and Heroes

The alleged divinity of Jesus is consistent with the hero cult common among peoples of the world who tell their stories often in the form of legends. For ancient peoples, a nation would not be great if its founder or hero appeared to be no different from ordinary folks. They therefore vest such people with divinity or super-human attributes that help to sustain their importance and mystique from generation to generation. In the case of kings, the investiture of divinity distinguishes them from their subjects and helps to perpetuate their dynasty and power. Belief in the divinity of kings was prevalent in ancient Egypt, Mesopotamia and Persia – regions very close to, and which had a lot of influence over, Israel. The ancient Egyptians, for example, believed that their king (Pharaoh) was not a mere human being but a manifestation of the gods and a mediator between the gods and the people.[56] According to the Encyclopaedia Britannica, Pharaoh was regarded as the sky god (Horus), the sun god (Re, Amon, or Aton), or the image of the gods:

As the incarnation of all that is divine, the Egyptian pharaoh was addressed simultaneously in inscriptions as Aton, Horus, and Re [...] Significant for Egyptian royal theology was the doctrine of the god-kingdom spanning two generations; each king ruled as King Horus and became Osiris (the father of

---

[55] https://www.cgg.org/index.cfm/fuseaction/About.FAQ/ID/251/What-Does-Non-Trinitarian-Mean.htm, emphasis in the original.
[56] See, WRF Browning (ed.) supra n 45, 287.

Horus, a fertility god and later god of the dead) after his death.[57]

Similarly, ancient Persians revered their kings as the incarnations of the Sun or Moon God,[58] just as ancient Romans saw their emperors, and members of their families, as gods or sons of god and built temples and alters in their honour.[59] Noting the pervasiveness and universality of the hero cult,[60] the Encyclopaedia Britannica states that:

> *A broader foundation for the divinity of the king is the view of the king as the son of a god, which can take on different forms. The first king has been regarded as a god and his successors as sons of the god in a number of societies—in Africa, Polynesia, Japan [...] Peru [...] Egypt, Mesopotamia, and Canaan [...].*[61]

The apparent refusal of Jews to partake in the emperor worship was part of the reason for their persecution by the emperors of Rome until Emperor Constantine put a stop to it after becoming a Christian.[62]

---

[57] http://www.britannica.com/EBchecked/topic/515559/sacred-kingship/38718/The-divine-or-semidivine-king.

[58] Ibid.

[59] This is referred to as the 'Imperial Cult'.

[60] *Encyclopaedia Britannica,* http://www.britannica.com/EBchecked/topic/515559/sacred-kingship.

[61] http://www.britannica.com/topic/sacred-kingship/The-divine-or-semidivine-king. For a discussion of the divine or sacred kingship in Africa, see https://www.encyclopedia.com/environment/encyclopedias-almanacs-transcripts-and-maps/kingship-kingship-sub-saharan-africa; W Fagg, *Divine Kingship in Africa* (British Museum Press, 2nd Revised edition, 1978)

[62] See WRF Browning, *Oxford Dictionary of the Bible* (Oxford University Press 2009) 99. See also M Peppard, *The Son of God in the Roman World: Divine Sonship in its Social and Political Context,* (Oxford University Press 2011); GF Chesnut, supra n 28, 87-93.

Even in these modern times, Rastafarians regard late Emperor Haile Selassie of Ethiopia as divine and their redeemer. They call him the Lord of Lords, the King of Kings and the Conquering Lion of the Tribe of Judah. They believe him to be a descendant of King Solomon of ancient Israel and the Queen of Sheba of ancient Ethiopia, and the second Jesus Christ.[63] However, and in spite of everything so far discussed, is the name Jesus really special or indicative of the status of messiah?

---

[63] See *Encyclopaedia Britannica*,
http://www.britannica.com/EBchecked/topic/491801/Rastafari.

CHAPTER 14

IS JESUS A NAME ABOVE ALL NAMES?

Therefore, God exalted him to the highest place and gave him the name that is above every name, that at the name of Jesus every knee should bow, in heaven and on earth and under the earth, and every tongue acknowledge that Jesus Christ is Lord, to the glory of God the Father. – Philippi 2: 9-11

The claim that Jesus is the Saviour rests partly on his name, which the Bible's New Testament indicates, denotes him as such. According to Matthew 1:21, Angel Gabriel told Jesus' mother to give him that name 'because he will save his people from their sins.' Is this claim correct? The New Testament also refers to Jesus as Immanuel, which means 'God with us'. Does this make him special or equate him with God?

Meaning of the Names Jesus and Immanuel

The name *Jesus* is a transliteration of the relatively common Hebrew name *Yeshua* or *Yehoshua* (anglicised as 'Joshua') which in Hebrew means, 'The Lord (i.e., Yahweh) is help or salvation'.[1] It is similar to the name 'Isaiah' and does not suggest in any way that the bearer is

---

[1] See note 1:1 of Matthew 1, *New Oxford Annotated Bible*, supra n 17, ch.2, 1748. See also *Catholic Encyclopaedia*, http://www.newadvent.org/cathen/08374x.htm.

the one who saves. Instead, it affirms the Jewish belief that salvation comes from Yahweh. Similarly, the name Immanuel means, 'Yahweh is with us'. However, it does not suggest that the bearer is actually Yahweh who had physically come to be with the people. Instead, it means an acknowledgement by the people that Yahweh, their God, is with them. This is consistent with the practice in many cultures of the world, where people give names to their children in praise, thanksgiving or glorification of, or otherwise signifying connection to, God. Such names never suggest that the persons who bear them are God or responsible for doing the things indicated in them, as many biblical examples illustrate.

The name *Isaiah* means 'Yahweh is salvation', but there is no suggestion that Prophet Isaiah was Yahweh or Saviour. The name *Ezekiel* means, 'God strengthens' but does not mean that Prophet Ezekiel was the God that provides strength. The meaning of *Elisha* (My God is salvation) does not signify that Prophet Elisha was God or salvation.[2] Other examples include *Hoshea/Hosea* (salvation), *Abijah* (my father is Yahweh), *Abimelech* (God is my father) and *Eliakim* (God rises). These names do not suppose that the bearers were salvation, God's literal children or the literal resurrection of God. Therefore, the name *Jesus* does not indicate that the bearer is the Saviour. Similarly, even if Jesus were called *Immanuel*, it would not indicate that he was God that had come to stay with the people,

---

[2] See generally, http://www.behindthename.com/.

though, as already discussed, the Immanuel prophecy was not about him.[3]

A Common Jewish Name

The name *Yeshua* or *Yehoshua* is neither special nor peculiar in Israel. Although Philippians 2:9-11 declares that God had exalted Jesus 'to the highest place and gave him the name that is above every name' at the mention of which everybody should bow and confess to his Lordship, that claim is totally unfounded. This is because many characters in Israel bore that name before Jesus of Nazareth, the most famous example being the Yehoshua (Joshua) that reportedly led the Israelites into the 'Promised Land'.[4] Others include Joshua of Beth Shemesh,[5] Joshua the Governor,[6] the three Joshuas in Ezra (including two priests) who returned from Babylon,[7] and Joshua the priest who assisted Hezekiah.[8] In addition, numerous high priests in the biblical history of Israel bore the name Yehoshua;[9] and the writer of the apocryphal Bible Book of Ecclesiasticus is apparently a certain Jesus (Yehoshua) ben Sirach.

There were also many people with the name Yeshua at the time of the New Testament and early Christianity, the most notorious of these being Jesus Barabbas (Yeshua bar Abba, which translates into 'Jesus

---

[3] See Chapter 1.
[4] See the book of Joshua in the Old Testament.
[5] See I Samuel 6:14.
[6] See 2 Kings 23:8.
[7] Ezra 2:2,36,40.
[8] See 2 Chronicles 31:15.
[9] See *The Jewish Encyclopaedia*,
http://www.jewishencyclopedia.com/articles/7689-high-priest.

son of the Father'), the insurrectionist murderer reportedly freed by Pilate in place of Jesus. In Corinthians, Paul complained about other apostles preaching about a different Jesus from the one he preached.[10] In fact, given its relative commonality, it is not surprising that some Jewish pseudo-messiahs did bear the name Yeshua or Yehoshua.

A Literary Matter

Many people may not be aware of the fact that *Jesus* stands for *Yeshua/Yehoshua* probably because the later name does not appear in the English New Testament. Please note that all the books of the New Testament were originally in Greek, from which they were translated into Latin. From Latin they were translated into English. The Greek Bible (Septuagint) transliterated Yeshua/Yehoshua to '*Ieosus*' to reflect both the Greek language and the male gender. The Latin Vulgate then renders the name as *Iesus*. The King James Version of the Bible, translated from Latin, originally adopted Iesus, but later editions rendered it as '*Jesus*', to reflect the changes in the English language, which had by then adopted the letter J in its alphabet. In fact, in the original King James Version of the Bible published in 1611, the letter J was not used at all. Since Jesus was supposedly born a Jew and spoke Hebrew or Aramaic, nobody in his supposed lifetime would have called him Ieosus, Iesus or Jesus. Instead they would have called him, *Yeshua bar Yehosef* – i.e., *Yeshua* son of *Yehosef*. It remains now to consider the reason behind the doctrine of Divine incarnation and its effect on humanity.

---

[10] See 2 Corinthians 11:4-5.

CHAPTER 15

THE PERSONIFICATION OF GOD

I believe in one God, the Father almighty [...] and in one Lord Jesus Christ, the only-begotten Son of God, begotten of the Father [...] begotten not made, being of one substance with the Father, through Whom all things were made: Who for us men and for our salvation came down from heaven, was incarnate by the Holy Spirit of the virgin Mary, and was made man [...]. – The Nicene Creed

The dogma of Divine Incarnation is an attempt to humanise or personify God. Not satisfied with God as an unseen spiritual force and phenomenon, human beings often wish to make God 'real' and tangible. This mind-set is evident in the ancient belief, including among the people of ancient Israel and neighbouring nations, of theophany.[1] As the Oxford Companion to the Bible states, 'the appearance of Gods and their involvement with humans are common motifs in ancient Near Eastern and classical mythology.'[2] In order fully to understand their pains and sufferings, some ancient peoples believed that God needed to descend from

---

[1] This is the belief in the manifestation of deities as humans who could be perceived with physical senses.

[2] BM Metzger and MD Coogan (eds.) *Oxford Companion to the Bible* (Oxford University Press 1993) 740.

heaven and dwell with them in human form. Moreover, in order to vanquish their enemies, or to save them from the burden and condemnation of sin, some ancients believed that God would come physically as a great warrior, deliverer or Saviour. However, the belief in divine incarnation has many inherent problems.

Problems with Divine Incarnation

The first problem with the belief is that it creates a multiplicity of Gods. If different Gods have been incarnating as different human beings, and if the incarnates of the Gods are also Gods, it follows that there are a multitude of Gods, often working at cross-purposes. In Christian theology, not only was Jesus a human being; he was also fully God, extant from the beginning of time. Yet the same Jesus, while on earth, repeatedly prayed to and called on 'God the father' for assistance, bequeathed his soul, and conceded superior knowledge, to him. After his ascension, Jesus allegedly sat (or stood) at the right hand of God, thus pre-supposing the simultaneous existence of two deities, in addition to the third person in the Trinity – the Holy Spirit. This situation is reminiscent of the belief by many cultures in the multiplicity of gods, with each being responsible for different aspects of life. It is inconsistent with the notion monotheism.

The second problem with divine incarnation is that it attaches to God the nature, character, weaknesses and limitations of human beings. Thus, God would see with eyes, speak with a mouth, and walk with legs, just as humans do. God would also get angry, jealous, tired, disappointed, prone to mistakes and regretful as humans do. For example, God allegedly conversed with others in heaven prior to the creation of the earth;[3] and came down physically to the earth in order to meet and speak with Adam, Eve[4] and Moses.[5] God also allegedly needed rest after the labour of creation.[6] However, spirits do not have to communicate verbally; they neither labour nor tire; neither do they need to be physically present in order to meet or communicate with people. God, being the supreme spirit,[7] cannot be limited as human beings are and would not be the equivalent of humans. Thus, although the Bible says that God created humans in his image and likeness,[8] it may be more appropriate to say that it is human beings who attempt to create God in their own image and likeness.[9] This is evident from the images and sculptures of different deities from different parts of the world.[10] The Bible often portrays God as a person prone to jealousy,[11] anger and frustration,[12] and liable to take rash and regrettable actions.[13] This God needs to be constantly reassured of his people's faithfulness and appeased through constant praise singing, worship, offerings and sacrifices. All these, despite the fact that anger

---

[3] See Genesis 1:26.

[4] See Genesis 3:8.

[5] See e.g., Exodus 3:4; 33:7-21; 34:1-27.

[6] See Genesis 2:2-3.

[7] See John 4:24.

[8] See Genesis 1:26-27; 9:6; 2 Corinthians 4:4.

[9] See S Morenz, *Egyptian Religion* (translated by AE Keep, London: Metheun and Co. Ltd 1973) 16-26.

[10] See e.g., P Wilkinson and N Phillip, *Mythology* (Doring Kindersley Ltd, London 2007); A Cotterell, *The Illustrated Encyclopaedia of Myths and Legends* (Marshall editions Ltd 1989).

[11] See Exodus 20:4-5; 34:13-14.

[12] See e.g., Genesis 6:5-8.

[13] See e.g., Genesis 9:11-16.

and jealousy are negative human emotions condemned by the Bible,[14] and that constant wanting of love and praise, are a sign of weakness.

Moreover, personification invests God with the human foible of vindictiveness – giving love for love and hate for hate. For example, after first promising Eli and his house that they would be priests for ever, God was said to have withdrawn the privilege after the sons of Eli took sacrificed meat out of turn, declaring that, 'those who honour me I will honour, but those who despise me will be disdained.'[15] The Bible is indeed replete with occasions where Yahweh supposedly promises or delivers great blessings and favour to those who love him and obey his commandments while foisting curses, harsh punishment or disaster on those whom he perceives do not love him or obey his commandments.[16]

The third problem is that a humanised God cannot be universal, but would be national, political, tribal, parochial or sectional. In this context, God assumes the identity of the people to whom he or she belongs, becomes sympathetic to the plight of his or her people, and hostile or indifferent to others'. Thus, Yahweh is an enemy of Egypt, Edom, Babylon, Persia, Assyria, Philistine, Amalek, Moab, Median, etc. In like manner, other peoples and nations had tribal, local or

---

[14] See e.g., Proverbs 27:4; James 3:14-16; 1 Corinthians 3:3; 13:14.
[15] 1 Samuel 2:30.
[16] See e.g., Leviticus 26; Deuteronomy 28; Numbers 25:13; I King 11:11; Psalm 50:23; Proverb 8:17; Jeremiah 18:10; Malachi 2:9; John 12:26.

national Gods that were unfriendly or apathetic to surrounding or opposing nations or communities.

The fourth problem is that a humanised God loses omniscience, omnipresence, and omnipotence. In Genesis, Yahweh, the personified God of Israel, was apparently unaware that Adam and Eve would 'sin' and eat from the so-called Tree of Knowledge. He was also apparently not aware that Cain would murder his brother, Abel; or that human beings would turn bad. He thus regretted creating them and resolved to destroy them and the world.[17] Similarly, Yahweh was not aware of the way Saul would behave and regretted making him king. In short, being regretful was a recurrent emotion of Yahweh in the Bible.[18]

An incarnated God is not an omnipresent God, being restricted as it were to a particular womb, family, village or nation during the different phases of the incarnation process. God carried in the womb of a woman for nine months would be nothing more than a foetus whose presence does not extend beyond the amniotic sac. God as a suckling, infant or toddler would have no presence beyond his immediate family or places where his carers choose to take him. God as a child would probably not travel beyond his village or city unless his parents or guardians take him with them on a trip. God as an adult would spend most of his time in the village, city and country of his birth; and in ancient times when means of transportation were severely

---

[17] See Genesis 6:5-8.
[18] See further, Genesis 6:6-8; Exodus 32:13-14; 1 Samuel 15:35.

limited, might only venture occasionally into neighbouring towns, cities and nations. This is true in the case of Jesus. The gospels record his ministry as taking place mostly in relatively small Judean towns and villages, especially those in the region of Galilee, with only occasional forays into the cities of Jerusalem (in Judea), Samaria (in Israel), and neighbouring areas. Unless there are multiple incarnations of God as different persons in different places at the same time, the incarnation of God in one place means its absence in other places. John's gospel sharply demonstrates this when it emphasises that Jesus Christ was the *only* begotten son of God, and the *only* name by which men would be saved.[19]

An incarnated God is also not omnipotent. God in the form of a foetus, an infant, or child could hardly wield any power; rather, it would be a whining, weak and helpless entity at the mercy of his parents or carers. God as an adult human being confined to one corner of the globe, would not wield much power either. In short, an incarnate God becomes a material, circumscribed and limited being rather than a spiritual, all-knowing and infinite power. Thus, the claim is utterly ludicrous that a woman could be the mother of God, as in the case of Mary and Jesus, Isis and Horus, etc.[20] It must have been the doctrine of incarnation that gave rise to the fanciful notion of divinity of kings.

---

[19] John 3:16.
[20] *Encyclopaedia Britannica*,
http://www.britannica.com/EBchecked/topic/515559/sacred-kingship.

An omnipotent, omniscient and omnipresent God does not need to come down from heaven or anywhere else to do anything, or to expend physical strength in order to make things happen. The mere wish of God should manifest the intended outcome anywhere in the universe. God does not have to be physically present in order to be cognizant of the pain, suffering and needs of people. God does not need to incarnate in order to deliver people from their oppressors or sins. If God wishes to deliver people, the deliverance happens, wherever the people might be. In any event, such a deliverance from sin is not necessary and does not happen.

An incarnate God is usually mortal since it might have to die in order to return to the Father God. In the case of Jesus, the Bible tells us that he died and remained dead for a number of days and nights before he resurrected and ascended to heaven. How could Jesus have been God while he was dead? The Bible insists that when people die they remain dead and oblivious of everything,[21] until the end of time when they would resurrect for judgment.[22] If Jesus were the full manifestation of God and the same as God, the implication would be that when he was dead and buried, God was also dead and unaware of anything.

Another problem is that incarnation makes God to need and have sons and daughters in the manner of human beings. The supposed incarnation of God as Jesus Christ comes with the twist that Jesus was the only begotten son of God. It is therefore especially significant that

---

[21] See Ecclesiastes 9:5.
[22] See e.g., Isaiah 26:19; Daniel 12:2; I Thessalonians 4:14; John 6:40.

God sent this precious son to the world to die for humanity – a point strenuously emphasised by the Bible.[23] It is ridiculous, however, to claim that God begot a son or an only son. To beget in this context means to bring into existence through the process of reproduction a 'fruit of the womb', a phrase used of Jesus,[24] whom the Bible insists was 'begotten and not created'.[25] Begetting is a thing of the 'flesh' not of the spirit. As the ultimate spirit and the creator of all things, God does not re-produce or beget as humans do, but creates or causes things to come into existence. Incongruously, the New Testament insists that the same begotten Jesus is part of the Divine Holy Trinity, was present at the beginning of time, and took part in creation of all things. Thus, the father did not pre-exist the son; and the son is the same as, and equal, with the father.[26] However, inherent in the notion of being begotten is the fact that the begetter or parent pre-dates, pre-exists, and supersedes the begotten or offspring. In any event, the notion of gods having spouses and children and the doctrine of the Trinity or multiplicity of gods are themes found in the mythology of many religions described as 'pagan'.[27]

Furthermore, the personification of God means that God gets a gender. Accordingly, God is male and therefore father in many religions, and Jesus was a man. It is perhaps because of this that Yahweh's purported

---

[23] See e.g., John 3:16, 18; I John 4:9.
[24] Luke 1:42.
[25] See John 3:16, 18. The dogma is reflected in the Nicene Creed.
[26] John 1: 1-3.
[27] See generally, P Wilkinson and N Phillip, supra n 10. On the doctrine of trinity in ancient Egyptian religion, see S Morenz, supra n 9, 142-146.

covenant with the Jews was only with men, and based on male circumcision. In some cultures, God (Goddess) is female, while in others there are different Gods, some male and some female, with the male and the female co-habiting to produce offspring. However, an all-powerful and all-knowing God is not confinable to any gender.

The next problem with the belief in the incarnation of God is that it erects a barrier and distance between humans and God implying as it were that access to God would be only through the incarnate. Therefore, the New Testament teaches that we can relate to God through Jesus, our only mediator and advocate before God. Meanwhile, adherents of Mithraism saw Mithra as the mediator between humans and God, while Hindus ascribe that role to Krishna. By this belief, God will not entertain or answer our prayers unless we pray through the incarnated intermediary. This teaching is false and prevents humans from deploying their enormous spiritual powers to realise their potentials. If God is everywhere, it follows that God is with every human being at all times and in all places. If the spirit of God is in every human being, it also follows that every human being is an aspect of God and able to interact with God without the need for any intermediary or advocate. While the assumption that humans need an intermediary between themselves and God – whether in the form of a redeemer, priest or minister – is very important and beneficial to religious institutions and leadership, it does nothing for the spiritual advancement of the laity.

Finally, belief in incarnation creates religious exclusivism and divisions. This is because the interposition of an intermediary and advocate between humans and God tends to undermine allegiance to God in favour of the presumed incarnate or mediator, and destroys the oneness and universality of God. Since respective believers of different religions would transfer allegiance to their own incarnated God, it means that God becomes different to people of different religions. Hence, for example, Lord Krishna, who is the incarnation of Vishnu, becomes different from Lord Jesus, the incarnation of Yahweh. Because of the above, the belief in the incarnation of God creates a feeling of religious specialness, superiority or exclusivism. If God had incarnated as the founder of a given religion to save humanity, there is an automatic implication that the religion is of God's making. It then follows that for people to reach God, they must go through that particular incarnate, with failure to do so occasioning hopelessness or eternal damnation.

The Bible, in many places, demonstrates this line of thinking by or in connection with Jesus. In John 14:6, Jesus reportedly said that he is the way, the truth and the life; and that no person could go to God, except through him. In John 3: 16 and 18, he declared that those who accept him as Lord would receive salvation while those who do not are condemned. On another occasion, Jesus assured his disciples that they have the keys to heaven, which would honour whatever they decree or do on earth.[28] Similarly, Jesus reportedly gave his disciples

---

[28] Matthew 16:13-19.

'all authority in heaven and on earth' and told them to make all nations his disciples.[29] Apostle Paul carries on this theme in Philippians 2: 9 – 11, when he says that God has exalted Jesus to the highest possible place and has given him a name above all others. Consequently, every knee in heaven and on earth must bow to Jesus and every tongue must confess that he is Lord. A logical implication of this claim is that God could only act through or in the name of Jesus, such that adherents of other religions and people without any religion will receive no favours from God.[30] This of course, is not the case.

Passages and claims like these and the belief they create logically justify a mind-set that those who accept Jesus as Christ are on the side of God while those who do not are against God. Indeed Jesus appeared to articulate this sentiment when he said that, 'he who is not with me is against me, and he who does not gather with me scatters';[31] and by the statements that those who do not accept his gospel are damned.[32] At best, this kind of sentiment creates a zeal to proselytise; at worst, it creates bigotry, separation and discrimination as demonstrated by the apostle Paul who enjoined Christians not to associate with unbelievers whom he considered synonymous with unrighteousness, wickedness and darkness.[33] This expression of religious exclusivism and bigotry is also prevalent in some other scriptures, including Jewish and Islamic, and is largely responsible for forced conversions

---

[29] Matthew 28:18.-19.
[30] See e.g., John 6:44; 14:6.
[31] Matthew 12:30.
[32] See e.g., John 3:15-16, 18-19, 36; 8:24; Mark 16:16; Romans.
[33] See 2 Corinthians 6:14.

and religiously motivated violence and terrorism. This is the bane of organised religion.

CONCLUSION

This book has endeavoured to reveal details of the story of Jesus Christ that are unknown to believers, but which are fundamental and vastly different from popular assumptions. The Bible's New Testament depicts Jesus Christ as both divine and human, and the Saviour of humanity. However, this book has shown that the stories about him – from his conception up to his ministry, death, resurrection and ascension – lack veracity, internal consistency and historical validation. Rather, they are attempts by Christian authorities and gospel writers to clothe theology in the garbs of fact and history.

The book has demonstrated that the story of Jesus Christ, as told in the New Testament, is as mythical as the stories of the heroes and god-men and god-women of many religions that pre-existed Christianity. Thus, the gospel of Jesus Christ is a quintessential religious narrative, the aim of which is to supplant Judaism and promote Christianity as the new paradigm for Divine-human relationship. This penchant is common among newer religions, which – though reliant on older ones – project themselves as the newest and last testament of God.

The purpose of this book is simple: enlightenment and empowerment of people through the revelation of the truth. The wish is that readers, especially those in developing parts of the world, would know that Jesus and his exploits exist only in the pages of the New Testament, and in their imagination and faith. Although, everyone remains free to believe whatever they want, belief is different from knowledge. Only knowledge can dispel ignorance and protect people from deception and exploitation. The time has come for human beings to focus on spirituality and knowledge of God and do away with retrogressive and divisive superstitions, myths and dogma.

BIBLIOGRAPHY

Acharya S, *The Christ Conspiracy: The Greatest Story Ever Sold* (Adventures Unlimited Press 2012).

Alighieri D and DH Higgins, *The Divine Comedy* (Oxford World Classics Paperback 1988).

Ancient History Encyclopaedia, http://www.ancient.eu.

Andrae T, Mohammed: The Man and His Faith (Dover Publications Inc. 2000).

Atwil, J, *Caesar's Messiah: The Roman Conspiracy to Invent Jesus* (CreateSpace 2011)

Barton J and J Muddiman (eds) *The Oxford Bible Commentary* (Oxford University Press 2007).

Bible, New King James Version (Collins, Box Lea edition 2011).

Bible, New Revised Standard Version (with Apocrypha) (Oxford University Press 2001).

Bible, New International Version (Hodder & Stoughton 2015).

Bible, New Jerusalem Version (Pocket Edition) (New York: Double Day 1990).

Bowker John, *Oxford Dictionary of World Religions* (Oxford University Press 1997).

Bradford AT, *The Jesus Discovery: Another Look at Christ's Missing Years* (Templehouse 2010).

Browning WRF, *Oxford Dictionary of the Bible* (Oxford University Press 2009).

Catholic Encyclopaedia, http://www.newadvent.org/cathen/.

Cavendish R (ed.), *Legends of the World* (Orbis Publishing Ltd 1982).

Chesnut GF, *Images of Christ: An Introduction to Christology* (Seabury Press 1984).

Cotterell A, *The Illustrated Encyclopaedia of Myths and Legends* (Marshall editions Ltd 1989).

Cross FL and EA Livingstone (eds) *Oxford Dictionary of the Christian Church* (Oxford University Press 1974).

Cross FM, *Canaanite Myth and Hebrew Epic: Essays in the History of the Religion of Israel* (Harvard University Press 1973).

Crossan JD, t*he Historical Jesus: The Life of a Mediterranean Jewish Peasant* (San Francisco: Harper 1991).

Crossley J, *Jesus and the Chaos of History: Redirecting the Life of the Historical Jesus* (Oxford University Press 2015).

Crystal, D (ed) *Penguin Encyclopaedia* (Penguin Press 2004).

Ehrman BD, *Whose word Is It? The Story behind who changed the New Testament and Why* (The Continuum International Publishing Group 2006).

Encyclopaedia Britannica, http://www.britannica.com/topic/creation-myth.

Evans SC, *The Historical Christ and the Jesus of Faith: the Incarnational Theory as History* (Clarendon Press, Oxford 1996).

Fagg W, *Divine Kingship in Africa* (British Museum Press, 2nd Revised edition 1978).

Fox RL, *The Unauthorised Version* (Penguin Books 1991).

Forsdick HE, *The Man from Nazareth* (New York: Harper & Brothers 1949).

Fitzgerald D, *Nailed: Ten Myths that Show Jesus Never Existed at All* (Lulu.com 2010).

Frazer JG, *Adonis Attis Osiris: Studies in the History of Oriental Religion* (London: Macmillan and Co. Ltd 1906).

Friedman RE, *Who Wrote the Bible?* (Harper Collins 1997).

Hastings J (ed) *Encyclopaedia of Religion and Ethics* (Edinburgh: T and T Clark 1971).

Humphries K, 'Nazareth: the Town that Theology Built', http://www.jesusneverexisted.com/nazareth.html.

Humphreys K, *Jesus Never Existed: the Tragic Fabrication of a Saviour of the World* (NineBanded Books.com; Jesusneverexisted.com).

Johnston SI (ed) *Ancient Religions*, (The Belknap Press of Harvard University 2007).

Josephus F, *Antiquities of the Jews* (Acheron Press 2012).

Josephus F, *The Wars of the Jews* (Palatine Press 2015).

Kuster V, *The Many Faces of Jesus Christ* (Neukirchener Verlag, 1999, translated by John Bowden 2001).

Goring R, *Larouse Dictionary of Beliefs and Religions* (Kingfisher Publications PLC, New ed. 1994).

Lumpkin JB, *The Life of Saint Issa, Best of the Sons of Man: The Missing Years of Jesus and His Travels in the East* (Fifth Estate 2012).

MacCulloch D, *A History of Christianity* (Penguin Books 2012).

Mackey JP, *Jesus the Man and the Myth* (SCM Press Ltd 1979).

Marshal L (Rev.) (ed) *The Mythical Life of Jesus* (Trafford Publishers 2011).

Massey G, *Gerald Massey's Lectures* (The Book Tree, California 2008).

Massey G, *The Historical Jesus and the Mythical Christ* (Forgotten Books) www.forgottenbooks.org.

Massey G, *Ancient Egypt, the Light of the World: A Work of Restitution and Reclamation in Twelve Books*, vol. 1 (Routledge 2013).

Metzger BM and MD Coogan (eds.) *Oxford Companion to the Bible* (Oxford University Press 1993).

Modeme LE, *Fantasy of Salvation* (Ameze Resources Ltd. 2019)

Morenz S, *Egyptian Religion* (translated by Ann E. Keep) (London: Metheun and Co. Ltd 1973)

Murdock DM, *Christ in Egypt: The Horus-Jesus Connection* (Steller house Publishing 2009).

Murdock DM, *Who was Jesus: Fingerprints of the Christ* (Stellar House Publishing 2011).

Myth Encyclopaedia, http://www.mythencyclopedia.com/Go-Hi/Heroes.html.

New Oxford Annotated Bible, NRSV with the Apocrypha (4[th]ed)
(Oxford University Press 2010).

O' Collins GSJ, *Christology: A Biblical, Historical and Systematic Study of Jesus* (Oxford University Press 1995).

Pack, 'Christ's Resurrection was not on Sunday', *The Restored Church of God*, http://rcg.org/books/crwnos.html.

Peake AS, *et al*, (eds.) *A Commentary on the Bible* (Nelson and Sons Ltd Edinburgh 1937).

Pearce Matthew, *Twelve Infallible Men: The Imams and the Making of Shi'ism* (Harvard University Press 2016).

Pepperd M, *The Son of God in the Roman World: Divine Sonship in its Social and Political Context (*Oxford University Press 2011).

Price S and E Kearns, *The Oxford Dictionary of Classical Myth and Religion* (Oxford University Press 2003).

Ranke-Heinemann U, *Putting Away Childish Things: The Virgin Birth, the Empty Tomb, Hell and Other Fairy Tales You Don't Need to Believe to Have a Living Faith* (Harper San Francisco 1994).

Ratzinger J (Pope Benedict XVI), *Jesus of Nazareth* (London: Bloomsbury Publishing plc 2007).

Renan E, *The Life of Jesus* (New York: Random house 1972).

Rosenberg D, *World Mythology: an Anthology of the Great Myths and Epics* (McGraw Hill Companies Inc. 1994).

Sahih-al-Bukhari (a collection of Islamic oral traditions), http://www.sahih-bukhari.com/Pages/Bukhari_1_07.php.

Sanders EP, *The Historical Figure of Jesus* (London: Penguin Books 1995).

Schweitzer A, *The Quest of the Historical Jesus* (New York: Dover Publications Inc. 2005).

Stanton G, *The Gospels and Jesus* (Second ed) (Oxford University Press 2002).

Thiering B, *Jesus the Man: A New Interpretation from the Dead Sea Scrolls* (London: Doubleday 1992).

Twelvetree G, *The Cambridge Companion to Miracles* (Cambridge University Press 2011).

Tyrell G., *Christianity at the Crossroads* (London: Longmans, Green & Co 1909).

Warner R, *Encyclopaedia of World Mythology* (London: BPC Limited London 1975).

Wells GA, *The Jesus Legend* (Chicago: Open Quest 1996).

White, EG, *The Spirit of Prophecy: The Great Controversy Between Christ and Satan*, Vol. IV, 1969 (Washington: Review and Herald Publishing Association 1969).

Wilkinson P and N Phillip, *Mythology* (Doring Kindersley Ltd, London 2007).

Wilson AN, *Jesus* (London: Sinclair Stevenson 1992).

Zeitlin IM, *Jesus and the Judaism of His Time* (Policy Press 1988)

INDEX

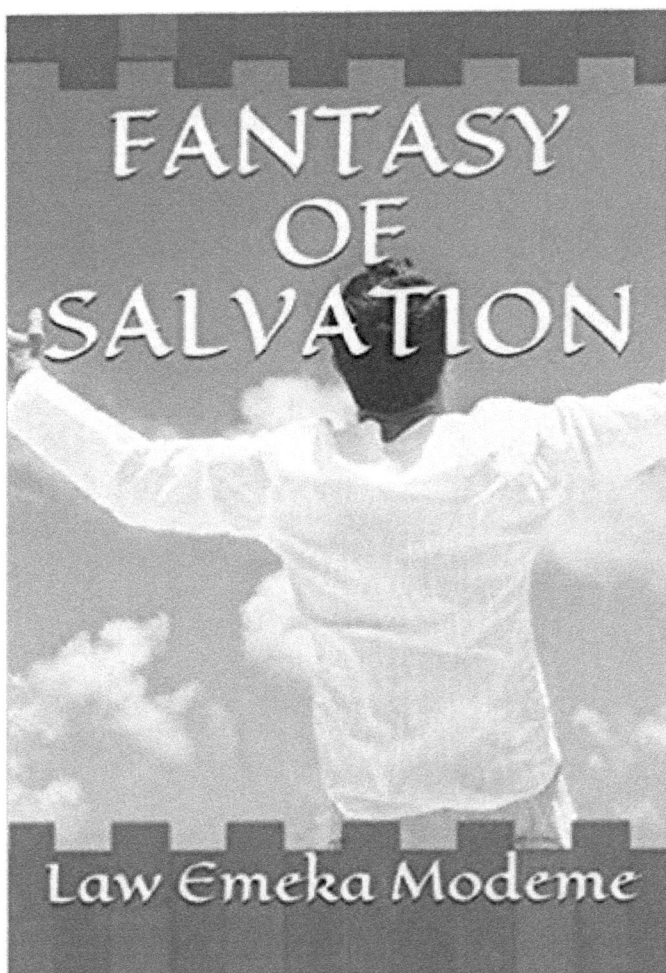

FANTASY
OF
SALVATION

Law Emeka Modeme